Whisky for Tea

WHISKY FOR TEA

Sir Hugh Ripley

The Book Guild Ltd.
Sussex, England

For Kate

The Book Guild Ltd.
25 High Street,
Lewes, Sussex.

First published 1991

Set in Baskerville
Typesetting by ABM Typographics Ltd.,
Hull.
Printed in Great Britain by
Antony Rowe Ltd.,
Chippenham, Wiltshire.

British Library Cataloguing in Publication Data
Ripley, Hugh
Whisky for tea.
1. Great Britain. Social life, 1901 – Biographies
I. Title
941.082092

ISBN 0 86332 637 4

CONTENTS

1

A Shropshire Lad

I have a very clear recollection of the day and night nurseries at Bedstone House, Shropshire, where all the family – three brothers and two sisters – were brought up. They were two spacious adjoining rooms, the day nursery having an assortment of large Victorian cupboards and chests of drawers and a huge dappled grey rocking horse. The bathroom and loo, a magnificent wooden affair with panelling each side and a chain pull with an appropriate picture of Vesuvius erupting, was situated at the end of a long dark passage. During winter evenings we were sometimes scared going down that corridor unless accompanied.

My cot-cum-playpen was a solid brown wooden bunk with vertical bars with one side that let down, although I was unable to operate the mechanism from the inside. Presumably all the family started off in this cot and there was a new occupant every three years or so. I certainly remember my sojourn there quite clearly. We were attended to by Nanny Watts, wife of the estate foreman, and a nursery maid by the name of Nora. I don't think my mother took a great interest in me at this time of my life. She was usually busy with domestic affairs, gardening and looking after her chickens. Besides this, she attended Petty Sessions in Bishops Castle and was a stalwart in the Women's Institute meetings as well as the fund-raising functions for the church held in the parish hall erected by my father.

At my christening in St Mary's Church, Bedstone, I was given the name Hugh only, although my birth certificate gives the names 'Hugh George Harley'. I never did discover whether they forgot the other names or whether they thought plain Hugh would suffice. Certainly I was no beauty: a prominent nose and a long face, with one solitary hair on my head. The family felt that I was destined to be a judge one day.

Once I had left the cot and got to the walking stage I was rather a disagreeable child. On walks with the nurse pushing the pram, and either younger sister Susan or younger brother Nigel aboard, my elder brothers and sister would rush on ahead and consider the whole thing a great adventure whereas I invariably trailed a long way behind and was scolded for not keeping up.

Although I spent my youth in Shropshire I can claim to be a Yorkshireman since I was born at the Bishops Palace, Bishopsthorpe, near York in 1916. Evidently the palace was requisitioned during the Great War and my father, who was in the Royals, had a Corps staff appointment there. I was always told that I was born at the time of German Zeppelin raids over Yorkshire.

In the post First World War days country life was conducted in a leisurely fashion. Compared with today it would indeed seem easy and even luxurious. Father was left the Bedstone and Hopton Castle estates which were adjacent, under the entail to the eldest son. They amounted to about five thousand acres, and, having no money, he lived off rents from tenants and timber sales. He rarely had any cash and never went around with his pockets stuffed full of cash like the business fraternity. When really up against it he managed to get a deed of disentail and sell off the odd outlying farm.

Although the tax situation in those days was not very severe his wages bill was not inconsiderable. The outside staff consisted of Hallet, the groom, and a stable lad and cowman; Nanny Watt's husband, Herbert, the estate foreman; Howells, the carpenter; Grub, the forester; and Owen the gardener, together with a boy. My father was also responsible for the inside staff, although my mother, a Harley from Brampton Bryan in Herefordshire, received a small dowry on her marriage and produced a little income from her chickens. Inside the house we were looked after by a butler, a parlourmaid, odd dailies, a cook and scullery maid, nanny and nursery maid – and, as we grew older, tutors and a French governess.

Father was brought up at Bedstone Court, a huge Victorian house of little architectural merit, close to Bedstone House and built by his grandfather, the first Bart, from money made in Bradford in the woollen textile business. However, the Court and pleasure gardens were out of bounds so far as we children were concerned because the place was let to Mr Langley (and afterwards to Mrs Foley). During the Second World War it was occupied by both boys' and girls' schools. Heatherdown at Ascot, under the stewardship of Mr Warner, was evacuated there.

My father was always approachable to the schoolboys and would usually stop and talk to them. Simon Broome, the former managing director of the Stafford Hotel in St James's, London, once told me that they had many discussions together when he was a schoolboy at the Court. He said that it could be a little disconcerting at times as father tended to carry a shotgun when he was wandering around the countryside and, in the middle of a conversation, was quite liable to loose off at a rabbit or a pigeon.

After the war I sold the Court as well as Bedstone House, which I considered to be untenable due to its proximity of the school, together with the Vicarage which I had just bought. Now the whole enterprise has developed into a successful co-educational public school which goes under the name of Bedstone College.

To the south of Bedstone House we had a grass tennis court which was mowed by Owen, the gardener, with the help of a boy pulling in front or sometimes a pony with special little leather shoes attached to its hooves. When Owen bent over to remove the grass cuttings his bum presented a lovely target for an air gun. He would leap into the air, curse, and then give chase. We were much more nimble of foot than the old gardener who could never catch us. My father eventually put a stop to this practice and I believed Edward, my eldest brother and always the ringleader of these pranks, got the strap.

Past the tennis court there was an area known as the long grass which was scythed twice a year, usually by my father who did it very expertly. To one side and in amongst mature beech and oak trees the guinea-pig house was situated. This contained all manner of livestock from pet rabbits and guinea-pigs to bantams, which wandered around the garden. At the top of this little building there was a dovecote for our pigeons. They were very tame and presented a pretty sight flying around the house.

Apart from the tenanted farms father kept a small home farm

in hand with a small herd of Jersey cows. Fresh milk, cream and butter were always available for the family and the people on the estate. As children we were all quite adept at milking cows and making butter in the dairy, although we didn't much care for the latter chore.

There was rather a nasty smell attached to the butter-making process and we considered it a job for the women, such as our sisters. Father always kept a Jersey bull, a breed notorious for its unpredictable temperament. The stock bull was usually kept inside and the cows were brought to him. Even young Jersey bulls should be given a wide berth and many a time we were chased, but we made sure we had an easy exit from the field. On one occasion the cowman who had reared the calves was attacked by a little fellow. Although the poor chap ran as fast as he could towards a gate the bull caught up and tossed him. Fortunately the bull was still fairly young and had not developed proper horns, so no great damage was done.

A flock of Kerry and Clun Forest sheep were kept on the hills. Edward was presented with a certain number of sheep and soon learnt a very good lesson with regard to safety precautions. He was shooting rabbits on one of the hills and fired at one as it was disappearing over the crest. At that precise moment one of his own ewes appeared over the top and he shot it dead. Naturally father remonstrated with Edward, saying that it might have been the shepherd or some other human being. It was a classic example of disobeying one of the fundamental shooting rules *i.e.* 'Never shoot where you can't see'. All things considered, it was just as well it was one of his own sheep.

We also kept pigs some way from the house at the back of the old farm buildings. Most of the little piggies went to market, but once a year one decent sized porker was slaughtered for home consumption. This was a great ritual and the village people turned up to witness the event, knowing that in due time they would be given lots of bits and pieces, such as scratchings and offal. Fortunately I was prevented from attending these proceedings. The wretched pig was laid out on a block where his throat was cut and he bled to death. The squeals sounded as if they could be heard for miles around. All I can remember was seeing the pig hung up by a home-made winch dripping blood into a bucket. After the killing we all lived well on various parts of the porcine anatomy, including the trotters, whilst the sides of ham and bacon were cured and eventually strung up on hooks in the larder, the kitchen and the scullery room.

Mrs Parker, the cook, baked bread in an old fashioned oven once a week and she always made us children baby loaves which we ate with relish while they were hot and crispy. If one went into the kitchen and particularly the scullery at night there was a rustling noise. Putting on the light, one could see a hoard of cockroaches scampering across the stone floor and disappearing down various crevices. This spectacle was particularly evident after a baking operation. Nowadays the sight of one cockroach – especially in certain clubs I could mention – gives most people the jitters and the local health authority is immediately alerted. But they never seemed to do us much harm.

The three boys, that is Edward, Derek and myself, always went around together. I was just tolerated and never showed any particular signs of leadership. We never bothered much about the youngest two, Susan and Nigel. They were good friends and kept together while Ruth, the second eldest, seemed to be quite happy sewing and doing domestic chores. Yet she was good on a horse and spent a lot of time with her own grey cob, called Joy, who jumped like a stag. Ruth loved her hunting and went well to hounds.

Ruth was a very kind and considerate girl. She would go out of her way to help others and was particularly good in the parish. I believe she had rather a sad life. She was plain and shy and I don't remember her ever having a boy friend although the family did their best to encourage romance with various young men who came to stay. In the Second World War she became a VAD and worked very conscientiously. Touching letters were received by my parents from doctors and nursing staff about her contribution during those difficult war years. She died of nefritis at Bedstone while quite young and is buried in the churchyard.

We all learned to ride at a very early age. Father, being an ex-Cavalryman, was determined we should all develop what he termed 'a good seat'. To achieve this we were made to ride bareback for a year. This is an excellent discipline. It creates a good sense of balance and probably good hands since you have no purchase to pull the horse's mouth. We passed Father's standard when we had successfully negotiated a series of jumps in the paddock.

We had a collection of ponies for all ages, which were mostly kept out to grass summer and winter. Dolly and Peggy were the two little ones on which we started – and my goodness they used to take the mickey out of us on the hunting field! Although they were perfectly quiet and well behaved at home, they became tremendously excited at seeing the hounds and being amongst other horses galloping around. The Welsh border country is full of steep hills and if they had the opportunity they would set off at full speed down a terrible gradient, with the one following the other. The best thing was to close your eyes and hang on with might and main. They usually stopped very abruptly at the bottom of the mountain.

Dolly and Peggy were crafty little devils who also tried to dislodge you when you were going through a wood at speed. They would purposely go under a low branch or, when steered, say, to the right of a large oak tree, they would at the very last moment switch direction and go to the left of it. Although there wasn't far to fall you had to keep your wits about you. Often we would go to meets five or six miles away on these little ponies and would end up at the far side of Stow Hill or some other Welsh mountain which entailed a hack back of about ten miles. Given their way, Dolly and Peggy would have galloped all the way back knowing that a nice warm bran mash would be awaiting them in the stables after a day's hunting. It was a long day. After rubbing down the ponies, Father insisted that we cleaned up all the tack and put it away in the harness room before settling down to boiled eggs and toast in front of the smoking room fire.

We would be out in the open air all seasons – sun, rain, snow or fog. It had its compensations. For example on a very wet and windy afternoon in the winter we would set off over the hills to Hagley Wood, about two miles away, where we knew pigeons were coming in to roost. Having placed ourselves in strategic position we would await the dusk with excitement and anticipation. Flocks of pigeons came in, swirling around against the strong wind preparatory to landing on the trees. This was our moment. We usually picked off a few, but the pigeon is a crafty bird and once we had had a few shots they would move to a safer place for a night's kip. Foggy weather is another excellent time to go after pigeons. They can't see you and fly low before coming in to roost. Furthermore they become disorientated and are unlikely to fly off to another wood miles away.

There was always great excitement at Bedstone when it started to snow, and we were all hopeful that it would continue to snow all night. Once there was a good layer, out would come the toboggans and skis and we would head for the Dunstalls, a hilly part of the estate which was more of a sheep run than anything else. Father was a good skier and while none of us were up to his standard, he was happy to give tuition and loved to see us have a go.

My mother had a nasty shock when watching us tobogganing on the Dunstalls. Most of the children had piled on to a large flat-bottomed Norwegian wooden sledge. The ground was very hard and icy with only a thin covering of snow. Under these conditions the sledge accelerated to a high speed until it hit a cart rut at the bottom of the steep slope. It then shot up into the air, hurling the children aboard in different directions. My mother was horrified to see that there was no movement whatsoever from any of them. She thought we were all dead and ran down the hill to the scene of the accident screaming her head off. By degrees we began to sit up in a very dazed condition. By good fortune none of us had suffered any injuries. We were merely winded, having temporarily passed out.

The main shoot on the estate was let to Mr Langley, tenant of the Court, so as boys we were only allowed to go after pigeons and rabbits and an occasional snipe in outlying bogs. We also picked up the odd pheasant on the boundary when the coast was clear. Father also very kindly rented a rough shoot some miles away over the border in Wales for us boys. We had to work hard for the bags which we shot which were usually in single figures and consisted of partridges, pigeons, rabbits plus an occasional pheasant.

I remember one very strange incident when walking up a stony grass hill in search of partridges. A pack of hunting weasels appeared from nowhere and came straight towards me. It gave me a nasty shock and I was not quick enough to let off a shot before they were under my feet and had passed on through. I was able to give them one barrel before they disappeared in a fold in the ground but never got one. I am told this was not a figment of my imagination; it is a fact that weasels will hunt in packs and I was fortunate to witness such an occurrence at close quarters.

In childhood Sundays were always very different from other days of the week. Rods, always put up and ready, were left in their stands. Guns remained in their racks and ponies were not disturbed – they were merely visited and given a carrot or some such treat.

Mother would go to early service for Holy Communion (Father considered it his duty to go to early service on Christmas Day and Easter Sunday only). At a quarter to eleven Vern Williams, the roadman and fast bowler for the village cricket team, would pull the bell at St Mary's, the tiny parish church at Bedstone – at which father was Patron of the Living and appointed the parson. At five to eleven Vern would get into a quick beat and the bell resounded with some degree of urgency. By this time Mother, Father and daughters would be half way up the hill towards the church. The boys would have a last-minute scramble to clean their hands and faces and brush down their Sunday suits. Jackson, the butler, would help here and set them off to catch up with their parents before the bell stopped. Woe betide any of the children who were late or failed to turn up. They would get the strap.

The family always sat in the front two pews, with Father in the front on the outside. He positioned himself there in order to be well poised to take the collection plate round during the last hymn. The pulpit was only a few yards away and overlooking our seats. The parson would climb the little spiral staircase before delivering his sermon. In spite of the close proximity Father would invariably doze off and would sometimes wake up suddenly, having emitted an audible snore. There was no electricity in the church so it was necessary for the organ to be pumped by a little boy. On occasions the youth would be day-dreaming and fail to pump. In consequence the music would not start up at all or come through in disconcerting waves. Margy, the old Vicar's wife, was usually at the organ and we children sometimes felt she played the hymns too slowly. On these occasions we would sing lustily away ahead of her in order to speed her up. Derek, whilst at Oxford, was the only member of the family who ever read the lessons.

Father's mother, Granny, who lived at Heath House in the neighbouring parish of Leintwardine, always took her seat with her companion at the rear of the church. Afterwards, she would come down to Bedstone House and walk around the garden, discussing the shrubs and flowers with Father who was a great expert. After a good old English luncheon of roast beef carved by Father from a huge roast sirloin, and Yorkshire Pudding, we would repair to the drawing room where Father went to sleep and we were all supposed to be quiet. We couldn't wait for him to wake up so that us boys with him could set off for the usual Sunday walk. Armed with good walking sticks and a pack of dogs, Father's two bitch Springer Spaniels which went everywhere with him, Gyp, a smooth-haired fox terrier, which belonged to me, Smut, Derek's black greyhound, Edward's Norfolk lurcher and sometimes a couple of hound puppies, we set off.

Our destination was Gripes Nest, Darky Dale, where Old Grubb, the forester and his wife lived. Father would walk along ahead with his two spaniels to heel to have tea and an hour's chat in the Grubbs' cottage. He was a fine old fellow with a grey beard and a great knowledge of all aspects of forestry, including a well-run nursery of young trees. The cottage was completely isolated, situated away up the Darky Dale Valley, by a stream, nestled in at the foothold of the mountains and could only be reached by foot. Mrs Grubb was a delightful old lady. She was small with a fattish, but handsome, wrinkled face and very kind smiling eyes. She loved to make us all at home and give us tea and home-made cake. The son, Jack, aged about fifty, was usually present. He was a big bloated fellow with a perpetual smile. He suffered from dropsy and was not quite all there – though perfectly harmless.

Whilst Father went on ahead, the boys had a fine time with their assortment of dogs hunting rabbits up the overgrown stream until they reached Gripes Nest. It was fine rabbit country and the dogs usually accounted for two or three bunnies.

Sometimes on a Sunday we would be invited by Granny to lunch at Heath House, a large seventeenth century house with attractive pleasure gardens and a walled garden. This was quite a formal affair, with a maid and parlour maid, suitably attired, in attendance. We were all on our best behaviour and turned out in our best clothes. The food, although it came a long way away from the kitchens, was always delicious.

Granny, a small, frail and a very good looking old lady, had a soft and kind demeanour, yet she always seemed to command great respect and attention. She continued to live a true Edwardian life. Besides her companion, Miss Hall, she had a full indoor and outdoor staff. Crewe, the head gardener, a man of impeccable taste and manners, had profound knowledge of his job. The gardens and box topiary were kept up perfectly and were a real pleasure to walk round. Within the walled garden the potted flower greenhouse was a joy to visit – with everything propagated by Crewe. The fruit and vegetable greenhouse was equally impressive and the produce invariably received first prize at the local flower show. Later on, after the Second World War, I requisitioned the walled garden as a market garden with Crewe in charge. This was quite a successful and satisfying operation for some years and was most helpful for tax reasons.

Willie Adams, the chauffeur, was another character of note. He was a simple fellow with a club foot. He was always most respectful and although a great gossip, attended to Granny's every wish and whim as if she were a queen. Edith, Willie's wife, had been a member of the household since she was a child. Although Willie kept a stately old Daimler in the garage, it was rarely used. They preferred to go around in a bright red Ford van, similar to the GPO vehicle. He was an extremely slow and cautious driver.

Old folk in those days were creatures of habit. At eleven am Granny was served with a half-bottle of vintage champagne and a caraway seed cake. I believe one was made for her each morning of which she only took a slice. In the afternoon she went for a drive and ended up at Park Cottage, Hopton Castle, where she took tea. This was a most attractive small black and white house. In later years our cousins, the Rodneys, lived there and indeed my mother, assisted by Margy Ellwood, spent the last few years of her life at this cottage.

We all have our embarrassing times and moments. As a very small boy I went off to the loo after Sunday lunch at Heath House. For a bit of fun I decided to depart from the 'lav', as we used to call it, through a little window. There was easy access to it by standing on the mahogany surround of the WC. The exploit was successfully accomplished and I went off on my own to explore the woods and outer parts of the gardens, forgetting that I had locked the door of the 'lav' when I went in. In the meantime Father had a call of nature and found the door locked or jammed. Other members of the family were summoned and they pushed against the door to no avail. The matter was then forgotten for the time being whilst they all went for a tour round the garden. I joined them and the conversation turned to the mystery of the locked loo door, whereupon the enormity of my crime hit me and I went bright red. Rather like a Bateman cartoon all eyes were on me and I had to confess. I was marched back to the little window and by climbing onto Edward's shoulders I managed to regain access to the loo, again with much shoving and pushing. It was a relief to unlock the door and even face Father's wrath.

I never learnt the origin of the household run on Boat Race day. Mother, Father and the children together with the staff including Mrs Parker, the cook – a huge woman – all set off on a pre-arranged run round the garden. This was on a handicap basis. The younger and more agile participants were scratch whereas the infirm and older entrants were given a start – Mrs Parker was given a generous start since her bulk prevented her from moving at speed, and she could be an obstacle when trying to overtake on narrow paths.

When everyone was in their allotted positions Father fired a gun and we all set off. The excitement was intense and no quarter was given – much bumping and boring took place since there was a good prize for the winner. The most tricky part of the course was a narrow path through a large high rockery. It was here that Mrs Parker came to grief and she went tumbling down over the rocks having been barged by one of the boys – who invariably won. At the end of this exploit there were many grazed knees and bruises – yet everyone entered into the fun of the thing and there were no recriminations. I particularly remember Nora, the nursery maid, screaming with excitement all the way round. She invariably came down once or twice and ended up with torn stockings.

When we were quite small the family used to take a little white-washed cottage on the Welsh seaside of Borth, in the old county of Cardiganshire, for about a month, and indeed on a sunny day we would sometimes motor over there for a day trip.

It was about seventy miles away and our nearest outlet to the sea, involving a beautiful journey following the Wye practically to its source in the Plynlimons. Once over this mountain range there was a certain spot, close to a little Welsh cottage, where we could see the sea in the distance for the first time. This called for a tremendous cheer from the children in anticipation of a good time ahead.

More often than not our cousins, the Birkbecks from Norfolk, would come and stay with us at the cottage at Borth. On these occasions we would hire the next door cottage as well. Their family of six corresponded almost exactly with ours and we used to pair off in our respective age groups. As children the weather conditions at Borth made not the slightest difference to us. More often that not it was raining with a strong wind but this did not prevent us from playing on the beach and swimming – indeed during the daylight hours we were never out of our swimming gear and we seemed quite impervious to the cold. On the rare sunny days there was no question of us lying on the sand and sunbathing. We were much too active.

The rocks at Borth were always one of the main attractions to us. When the tide was out there were hundreds of little pools inhabited by lobsters, crabs and shrimps. On our return in the evening we had usually collected enough food for supper besides a few wounds on the feet from jagged rocks – Iodine and sticking plaster was always to hand and we were attended to by Mother or our sisters. On one occasion, Edward, paddling around in a little pool, had his big toe nipped by a lobster. In spite of waving his legs in the air the lobster would not let go. His brothers thought this was hilariously funny and their only concern was that the lobster should be safely landed. He was directed to a dry part of the rocks and the lobster was captured. Poor Edward hobbled around for a few days afterwards.

To the north of Borth towards Aberdovey, renowned for its sinking sands, we had many enjoyable adventures playing around in the sand dunes. Since the golf course was alongside we kept an eagle eye on wayward golfers and made quite a killing in retrieving lost balls.

In my early years before going to Eton, John Rocke was my best friend. His father, Evan Rocke of Clungunford, owned the estate practically next door. Of all the children round about, I seemed to be the only one who could get through to Squire

Rocke, a huge man with a red face. He was a difficult old fellow so far as his son was concerned and would not allow John to roam around the countryside in the way we did at Bedstone. Yet he had a good humour and always amused me. Further I remember him saying that I would live a charmed life and be lucky and successful.

All Squire Rocke's farms were let and in rather a dilapidated state. He never seemed to bother about them much apart from collecting the rent, yet he was a real expert at attending to his apple and other soft fruit trees in their large walled kitchen garden. At the time when the buds were beginning to sprout, you could be sure he would be down there, concealed with a gun on the look-out for bullfinches. They were his *béte noire* and he accounted for many. I do not think he was ever interested in pheasant, duck or partridge shooting, being much more interested in dealing with the bullfinches in order to ensure a good crop of fruit later on.

More often than not, John would bicycle over to see me and we would spend the day shooting, fishing or riding one of the ponies. Sometimes I would visit him at Clungunford, having borrowed a bicycle from John Marsh, son of the local tenant farmer. I never remember having a bicycle of my own. Situated towards the tail end of the family, I had to make do with cast-offs, including clothes from my elder brothers.

At Clungunford we were forbidden by Squire Rocke from going into the woods or visiting the nearby lake – presumably because we might disturb the game (duck and pheasant). So we spent some time playing around in the village. At a corner house just outside the Rockes' driveway gate we always knew we were likely to encounter a bit of trouble of an unusual nature. The occupants kept a pet magpie which was much more efficient than any watch dog. If we got too close to the wicket of the cottage the magpie would hop out into the road screeching and attack us. Fortunately it always went for our legs, but was most persistent and could give a nasty nip. It invariably held the floor and we had to retreat.

John Rocke, like his father, was a big boy and very mechanically minded, rather unusual for a country squire's son. When he was a little older and as soon as the law permitted, he acquired a large motor bike – a twin carburettor Ariel. This was my first experience with motor bicycles and I was to cover many miles on these machines later on. John was in a reserved occupation during the 1939-45 war years making aeroplanes near Bristol and thus contributing to the war effort.

Geoffrey Gwyer was another friend I sometimes spent the day with during the holidays. The Gwyer family lived at Eywood near Titley in Herefordshire. A huge Queen Anne house remodelled by Smirke in the nineteenth century for the fifth Earl of Oxford and Mortimer, it was alas demolished in the 1950s. The Gwyers had bought the place, long the seat of the Harleys, in the 1890s. I believe Geoffrey's father was a rich banker of Russian extraction; Geoffrey's Aunt Rachael (my godmother) married my uncle Ralph Harley of Brampton Bryan. Besides enjoying the company of Geoffrey, I looked forward to my visits to Eywood because I was always given a pound note – quite a handsome present in those days! Mr Gwyer senior was an interesting old boy and I had to be on my best behaviour. He had a rather disconcerting twitch and his head would suddenly shoot sideways while talking to you. Strangely his daughter Grace, sister of Aunt Rachael, had exactly the same affliction.

There was a pretty little stream meandering through the lovely grounds of Eywood. This is where Geoffrey and I would spend most of our time looking under the stones for crayfish. Although only the size of a mini-lobster, they had claws and could give a nasty nip. I suspect many unpolluted streams hold fresh water crayfish, but they are never seen unless you dig around for them. On each excursion we usually collected a bucketful and they made delicious eating.

2

Brockhurst

Nowadays little toddlers are taught the three Rs at nursery schools and local day schools and at that age it is established that they assimilate knowledge very rapidly. Although there was a perfectly good village school at Bedstone it was not considered by our parents to be a suitable place for us children to attend. Consequently, we were taught by a series of governesses, tutors and even the local vicar.

While a certain amount of discipline prevailed in our make-shift class rooms, we were able to get round our various teachers and continue to do what we liked best, such as looking after our pets and roaming around the countryside. As a result, and I don't think through any particular fault of our parents, we were very much less advanced than the modern child of today. I was scarcely able to read when I went to my prep school aged about eight.

Apart from staying with my cousins the Birkbecks at Westacre in Norfolk, where lessons were resumed in much the same way as at home, I had not been away on my own. Although preparations had been going on for some time, such as going through the school list and the packing of the trunk (this I had rather enjoyed since I was the recipient of a few new clothes for a change), I received a terrible shock when I was delivered to Brockhurst Preparatory School, Church Stretton, near Shrewsbury.

My mother had fortified me with a large tin of Mackintosh's toffees and a bag of wrinkled apples from the orchard. I was very tearful at the parting and was painfully homesick for quite a time – indeed at the start of each term I suffered from the same trouble. At my prep school I at least had my friend John Rocke, who was an exact contemporary. All through my time there we vied with each other to avoid being bottom of the form. Nigel Rodney, a cousin, was also at Brockhurst with us. He was of quite a different calibre and was usually top of his class.

R.P. Marshall, the headmaster, was not cut out to teach fairly thick boys, or to put it more charitably 'late developers'. He had an uncontrollable temper and instead of trying to understand the boy and using patience, he would resort to physical assault. If a boy displeased him, he would slap him on the face with all his force. Another torture he favoured would be to come up from behind and tweak an ear, screwing it around in a most painful way. He met his match once with an Irish boy called Minchin who was equally hot-tempered. R.P. had delivered a full-blooded smack on his face, which echoed around the classroom, whereupon Minchin in a state of fury picked up his inkwell and hurled it at the headmaster. He scored a direct hit and covered the bully in ink. Minchin was, of course, summoned to R.P's study later in the day and given six of the best.

If a headmaster resorts to physical abuse, it sometimes follows that an assistant master follows suit. Certainly this was the case at Brockhurst with two or three of them.

As I came from quite a musical family, it was decided that I should take piano lessons. This only lasted a short time. If I hit a wrong note when doing scales or practising a very simple tune, Mr Lambert, the music master would hit me smartly under the knees with a ruler. Wearing shorts and having no protection this was a most painful punishment and I used to dread going to my piano lessons. After suffering for two terms, I prevailed upon my parents to cancel my regular music lesson.

Apart from homesickness, punishments and so forth, I had a good time with my little friends, climbing trees. I was known as the 'monkey' since I was quite adept at that sort of thing and we used to build little dens in Brock Wood alongside. Sometimes I would leap on to a little pony which grazed in the nearby field and would gallop around bareback and without a bridle – much to the amazement of my little colleagues.

One Sunday afternoon I remember with a certain amount of disgust. Three or four of us boys went out for a walk and ended up in a little cattle shelter way out in the country. We decided to have a smoke. We had acquired a few cigarettes and made some extra ones by rolling up leaves. On our return to school for tea I was sitting next to Mr Lambert (the music master) and suddenly felt extremely ill. I was violently sick over the table. I was sent out of the dining room straightaway and Mr Lambert rushed out at the same time. Having recovered in the Common Room, I looked out of the window towards the master's bungalow situated on a hill about a quarter of a mile away where I observed Mr Lambert being very sick indeed over the edge of the bungalow garden. I thought to myself this will serve you right for being unkind to me during music lessons.

During the summer term, Mr Harry, the maths and games master, had considerable difficulty in teaching me to swim. There was a delightful little swimming pool at the top of the hill behind the master's house. The water was usually very cold, but we didn't mind this since we had a cold bath every morning throughout the year so that we all went well and truly under. In the swimming pool we wore red 'flogger pants' which were made of cotton and resembled the bottom part of a girl's bikini – you put one leg through, pulled them up and tied the tape on the other side.

Mr Harry spent many weeks holding a pole with me at the end with a strap around my middle. In spite of continually issuing instructions I made no progress and remained something of a water funk. In exasperation one afternoon instead of giving me the pole treatment he picked me up and threw me into the deep end. This did the trick. I set off for the other side and made it without any help. I had learnt to swim! Later I became something of a star turn and invariably won the diving competition. In fact I more than held my own in the games department, being captain of cricket and soccer and vice-captain of rugby. I became quite a big fish in a very small pool as I was to discover later at my public school.

R.P., the head, had two rather pretty and sexy daughters. Nora the eldest was too old for us (probably in her late teens) and was not at all interested in us little boys. But Barbara was about our age or perhaps a little older and beginning to blossom out. She did lessons with us and entered all the sports along with the other pupils. John Rocke and I were her special friends and we became quite familiar with her at our den in the wood or in the long grass on the edge of the playing fields. So far as I was concerned it never went much further than a bit of groping, but I often wondered if John went all the way. He sometimes seemed a bit sheepish after a lone excursion with her.

On the work side there was no improvement at all. All knowledge seemed to pass me by and provided I was having a good time the necessity of getting to grips with lessons never occurred to me. Of course the inevitable happened when faced with the Common Entrance examination – I failed dismally. Father was concerned about this episode in my life, particularly as Edward, his eldest son, had failed to get into Eton despite cramming and tutors. Evidently Father thought that I had the potential to pass the entrance examination if I were directed properly and made to work hard. So I was sent off to Mr Townsend who ran a crammer at Burnham-on-Crouch in Essex. I was not there very long, but by goodness he made me work. In fact I quite enjoyed it, probably because the other boys seemed to be even thicker than I was. I was considered to be the star pupil and was given special privileges such as going off into the town in a taxi to collect tuck for the boys.

Mr Townsend seemed to understand backward boys and had tremendous patience in spite of having a very nervous disposition. His stimulants took the form of endless cups of tea and cigarettes. He had piles of old Common Entrance exam papers and we had many trials before we sat for the proper examination. I have a strong feeling he crammed us on a hunch of what questions would be asked. At any rate, when the time came the questions had been well covered and I sailed through into Eton missing the bottom form!

Being an 'OE' himself, Father was tremendously pleased about my modest achievement and gave me a beautiful little pony – about fourteen hands – called Magpie. I believe it had been selected by Harry Birkbeck Senior – father's brother-in-law from Westacre, Norfolk. It was a well-bred looking chestnut with good speed and jumping ability – rather different from the cobs in the Welsh border country. I was very proud of Magpie, who went extraordinarily well in the hunting field. Together we were often successful at local gymkhanas.

3

The Ripley Tribe

My Father had a great influence on us boys as we grew up. Being a true countryman he joined us in all country pursuits such as shooting, hunting, fishing, cricket, tennis, golf and he had a very good knowledge of flowers and shrubs, knowing the Latin names. Under his influence we were always encouraged to be observant about nature whether it was identifying trees and wild flowers or knowing the call of wild birds.

When he had finished his days at Eton, Father joined the Royal Dragoons – now the 'Blues and Royals' of the Household Brigade. He saw service in the Boer War and in France during the Great War, where he was mostly attached to the Corps headquarters. Certainly he took out with him his two favourite horses, Rosie and Tinker, who left their marks in the paddocks at Bedstone by stripping most of the bark off a line of walnut trees. Fortunately the trees have survived although the trunks are still scarred. Tinker was a wonderfully bold small black horse who would jump anything in the hunting field, yet I imagine quite a handful to ride. We were never allowed on him.

Father married Dorothy Harley, daughter of the adjoining landowners at Brampton Bryan, and his sister Freda married Geoffrey, the eldest Harley son. Geoffrey was a huge man, six foot seven inches tall and a great friend of Father's. They went on trips shooting big game in Africa and salmon fishing in Norway. When competing in the cross-country race at Eton, the last obstacle was a deep brook, known as the River Jordan; most of the competitors would splash and swim through, indeed some dived in, but Geoffrey tried to clear it and landed on the steep bank and dislocated his hip. He had a pronounced limp ever afterwards. He died in his forties of pneumonia.

Father retired from the Royals as a captain to devote his time to running the estate and to fulfil the usual public duties which were expected of him. He was a magistrate and county councillor. In fact he was a very popular 'county bart' and was particularly kind and generous to all the tenants. His brother Guy, who lived in part of Heath House, acted as his agent for quite a number of years and had his estate office at the Heath. Guy was a proper 'country gent' too and, unlike Father, meticulous and efficient in everything he undertook.

In consequence a great deal of money was spent on farm buildings and houses to keep them in good condition – quite right in principle – but expenditure outstripped income from the property. So Father became poorer and poorer, particularly when faced with the educational expenses of six children. Fortunately for him the Bedstone estate was very well wooded and he was permitted to sell off timber, which he did to cover our educational expenses. Yet he always replanted. Guy and many others of the Ripley tribe received income from the Bradford Trust (Mill Property) but Father was excluded, since it was thought the agricultural income would suffice. He virtually had no other source of income.

None-the-less, despite financial problems, bank overdrafts and so on, Father carried on in his usual flamboyant way and was a very good companion to us boys. He invariably wore a buttonhole in his lapel and was never without a bright silk handkerchief. When he went out he was inclined to wear a boater, with MCC ribbon, a pair of 'co-respondent' shoes and a bow tie. He had a great love of motoring and for many years had a succession of large American touring cars such as Dodge, DeSota, Chrysler and Buick. He reckoned they were more advanced than the run-of-the-mill British cars and they certainly had much better acceleration. Father liked speed – something appreciated by us children on our returns from school. There was also a small run-about, usually an Austin or Morris Minor, which my mother drove – very badly.

Apart from holidays, sometimes with a caravan, and odd trips to the seaside at Borth, Father had three annual trips on his own. In May he would set off with his two spaniels in the boot of the car to Harrogate, staying at the Old Swan Hotel, to take the water. Later he would go up to London for the Ideal Home Exhibition, probably taking in some cricket at Lords and finally the Motor Show which he never missed. In the early days for these excursions he would stay with his sister, Freda, at 5 Walton Place (alongside Harrods) and, knowing most of the night clubs in town, he usually came staggering back in the early hours – no doubt the reason why my mother did not accompany him on these jaunts. In later years he made his headquarters at the Hind's Head, near the river at Bray, travelling to and from the exhibition by train.

Apart from his little holidays father lived quite a frugal life at home and to some extent lived off the land. There was game which he shot; trout which he caught in the river; chicken, eggs, which were organized by mother, while milk, butter, pork and mutton came off the estate; and vegetables and fruit from the kitchen garden. Father never seemed to have more than a pound or two in his pocket, used for drinks and petrol for his car. For more expensive items he would charge to his account to pay later – indeed he had accounts with most of the tradesmen in the neighbourhood.

One thing Father did not stint himself on was keeping his cellar at Bedstone House well stocked up, particularly with vintage port. Originally he bought pipes of port which were shipped over from Oporto and bottled in the cellar – a huge warren of a place – and left to mature for some years. He had acquired an uncanny knowledge of port and could invariably tell the shipper and the year of the vintage. A bottle of port was decanted every day and drunk after dinner, helped out in a modest way by us children. The boys in the family were given a glass at a very early age. The key of the cellar was very safely guarded and was only accessible to Jackson, the butler. It was out of bounds to us boys unless accompanied.

During the 1939-45 war years living standards at Bedstone House declined dramatically. Most of the staff left for war service or other reasons and they virtually lived from hand to mouth – although there was no shortage of local produce. Jackson remained on although he got into serious trouble. Father, being accustomed to his daily bottle of port, was told one day that there was none left. He quite unjustly flew into a rage, accused Jackson of drinking it and fired him. All the family were quite certain that Father had failed to check the stock and had drunk it himself. The family rebelled at this rough treatment of Jackson, so a compromise was reached that he would be demoted to outside duties only. So the poor old chap, instead of working in the butler's pantry and going around the house in his tailcoat and striped trousers, now could be seen outside in a pair of old cast-off tennis shoes doing the menial tasks such as stoking the boiler, clearing the rubbish away and feeding the chickens. He was not all that young either and suffered quite severely from rheumatism.

Like Captain Mainwaring in *Dad's Army*, Father, at the outset of the Second World War, became a platoon commander in the Home Guard. Early on they had a most strange collection of weapons from shotguns to old sporting rifles. As time went on and stores came through everything, including rifles, ammunition and grenades, was bundled together under the billiard room table. He would be out most evenings to meet his troops at a pub, where they had a very jolly time, before despatching them to their night observation duties on various prominent features within his area.

My mother, born Dorothy Harley, had an aristocratic pedigree as long and ancient as anyone in the neighbourhood. She was related to the politician Robert Harley, first Earl of Oxford and Mortimer; Harley Street, in Marylebone is one of the many tributes paid to him. Lord Rodney, the famous Admiral, was another of her ancestors. In those days the prominent county families usually married within their own social structure so Mother was related to most of the 'Lords of the Land'. She was deeply religious, going to Communion and Matins services most Sundays. Father did too, but he attended mostly as a matter of duty and to hand the collection plate round. Certainly we were all brought up very strongly in the Christian faith. Mother was musical and played the violin quite well; indeed we often had a musical evening when we all played our various instruments – except for father, who usually went into another room.

Riding side-saddle on her skewbald horse Mother usually set a good and independent line in the hunting field and she was a bold rider often prepared to tackle a large 'Bullfinch' hedge without any apparent anxiety. Having very little money of her own and, I suspect, an inadequate allowance from Father, she always gave the impression of being very mean. On reflection, I believe she was merely being careful in the housekeeping department. The storeroom was always locked up and the key hidden, and the same applied to the linen room. I never remember her doing any cooking.

She was more of an outside person and spent a lot of time in our large garden. Mother and Father would spend hours together rearranging the herbaceous border and planting annuals in the spring – yet he would spend most of his time in the rockery and attending to shrubs. Neither of them was particularly interested in the vegetable garden. The gardener looked after that and brought some produce into the house each day. As children we never really understood their devotion to gardening, although we were co-opted from time to time, and indeed enjoyed carting their refuse in a wheel barrow to the rubbish dump.

In order to make ends meet Mother kept a flock of free range chickens in the farm outbuildings. Their diet consisted of Indian corn scattered about in the morning and a bucketful of household scraps, mixed up with bran in the evening – the demoted Jackson used to help her in this department. She made a bit on the side by selling surplus eggs and the odd fowl. Sybil Birkbeck, Mother's younger sister, always remained close to her and as a result the children of each family saw a lot of each other in our youth. They were particularly good for us children, fixing up boys' cricket matches, tennis tournaments, dances and hunt balls.

My eldest brother Edward, heir to the baronetcy, was always the favourite of the family. He was a good looking, robust fellow – over six feet tall – and was brought up to inherit the estate and he knew every inch of it, yet he was not spoilt. He was a natural leader and as children we all looked up to him and followed him. Edward was a great sportsman, pretty good at all games. He was quite wild in his youth and always adopted a 'devil may care' attitude. There is no doubt he was fairly thick academically, having a succession of tutors during the holidays including Mr Shackleton, the vicar.

He evidently enjoyed his prep school, St Peter's Court, Broadstairs, and was well liked – indeed one of the masters, Linford, became his friend and stayed at Bedstone from time to time. However he failed his common entrance exam to Eton and instead went to Stowe. He and his great friend 'Shaggy' Carter were amongst the early intake to the school under J.F. Roxburgh. This former ducal estate proved to be just the place for Edward in the midst of some beautiful countryside in

Buckinghamshire. He and Shaggy spent a great deal of their spare time rabbiting and shooting. History does not relate how he got hold of a shotgun.

On one occasion he had a near squeak with the great headmaster. Edward, returning with Shaggy from an illicit shooting expedition, happened to run into Roxburgh. He had the barrel of the gun stuffed down his trouser leg and the butt wedged in his armpit whilst Shaggy was concealing game; consequently they were unable to doff their hats as they were supposed to do when encountering a beak. Roxburgh smiled at the two boys but never challenged them. There is no doubt the headmaster understood their predicament since there was little that went on in the school of which he was unaware.

After Stowe, Edward joined the county regiment, The King's Shropshire Light Infantry, through the Supplementary Reserve and spent two or three years in India before the Second World War. He was very popular with his brother officers and the regular Army suited him down to the ground. Joining the KSLI myself during the war I had a difficult act to follow – his name was always mentioned – so it took quite a long time for me to earn my spurs, in my own right, with the Regiment. During the early war years Edward commanded a depot in Shrewsbury, indeed I was a private under his command for a time. One summer evening when on guard duty I took great pleasure in prodding him with my bayonet. He was returning in high spirits in tennis gear I remarked, 'Its all right for some, how about the poor bloody soldier.' I also got my own back on payday. When it came to my turn in the queue the paymaster clerk announced the amount due to me. I said it was not enough and that he owed me five pounds and stood my ground. With all the Company present Edward decided against making a scene and paid up.

From his fairly cosy job at the depot in Shrewsbury Edward was selected to become a battle school instructor. This was a tough assignment which involved Commando-type operations under battle conditions using live ammunition. He became Chief Instructor under General Montgomery's command. Now that time was drawing near for the D-Day landing in Normandy in 1944, Edward was given command of a battalion in the Welsh Regiment. I have little knowledge what transpired during that period since I had been shipped off to

North Africa with the 1st Battalion of the KSLI and on to Italy when that campaign had been completed. It was then that I received the tragic news that Edward had been killed in the battle for Caen.

Derek, the second eldest son, was quite a different character to Edward. He was more serious and studious. He was not so robust physically, but he remedied this by body-building exercises; in fact he was quite a fitness fanatic and developed into a strong young fellow, well proportioned, and with an excellent physique. He was a good all-round sportsman and particularly crafty with a fishing rod. At school he was considered to be an intimidating fast-bowler, and was also a useful soccer player, being in the first eleven at Repton. He was always a sharp dresser – some of us thought not always in the best of taste – but he was proud of his wardrobe and liked to look smart. He spent much of his spare time strumming away at his guitar. In fact he was probably the most musical of the family and had a fine collection of operatic records. This served us well and was the foundation of my enjoyment of classical music.

He went to the same prep school as Edward, St Peter's Court, Broadstairs and, like the rest of the family, failed his common entrance at the first attempt. He was due to go to Dartmouth and make the Navy his career. Instead he went to Repton where he distinguished himself as a useful all-rounder. Father felt Derek had enough potential to go to a university so he was sent away to a crammer. Besides being a very kind and considerate fellow Derek was a hard worker and tenacious. He duly passed the exam and was admitted to Christ Church, Oxford. Unlike a number of his fellow undergraduates who were more interested in having a good time there he took his studies seriously with the intention of getting a law degree.

In his spare time Derek continued to play soccer. He also did some beagling, and joined the Oxford Auxiliary Air Squadron, where he duly won his wings. Throughout he had a steady girlfriend called 'Tisshie' and the two of them quite often came over to visit me at Eton and took me out to tea at the half-timbered Cockpit or I rustled up something in my study. When the undergraduates went down Derek continued his studies over the vacation at Bedstone. The billiard room and library were augmented by a collection of law books which he studied each day. He was duly rewarded by a good law degree.

For some reason or another he had an urge to go out to Borneo and hopefully work there. This was not to be. Instead he took a job on the Sudan Government Cotton Plantations and remained there until the outbreak of the war. He evidently enjoyed the life out there and played polo for recreation. When war was declared in 1939 he was immediately called up for flying duties in the RAF after his experience at Oxford. He was sent off to Habbaniya in Iraq for a training course on fighters. It was many years later, and quite by chance, that I discovered the Squadron Leader, Ken Osborne-Young (who took a gun in our shoot at Bedstone), was with Derek as an instructor, 'B' Flight no 4 Training School. Although Derek was a pupil of Dan Cremin, the Flight Commander, Osborne-Young did take him out on one occasion in a two-seater Hawker Hart bi-plane practising take-offs, landings and instrument flying. He remarked that Derek was much more advanced than the usual pupils at that stage.

I had not seen Derek since his Oxford days. Our paths did not cross. We were both carrying on with our respective careers, he in the Sudan, I on a tea estate in Ceylon, at the outbreak of the war. It came as a dreadful shock for me, having returned to England and having become a platoon commander in the 1st Battalion of the KSLI at Old Bolingbroke, Lincolnshire, to receive a message that he had been killed in action. From Habbaniya Derek had joined 80th Squadron in the Middle East. There had been nine RAF fighters against fifty Fiats and in two months they had accounted for forty-seven Italian planes. Derek and Squadron Leader Hickey were shot down on the same engagement. It was reported that Hickey parachuted safely from his plane. Then a Fascist machine-gunned him on the way down. It was also reported that the Greeks buried the two of them together just below the snow-clad mountains where they fell, believed to be in the area of Argyrocastro. Their names are inscribed on the war memorial at El Alamein but the War Graves Commission report that they have no known graves. Enquiries are still continuing to discover their actual burial place.

Indeed all members of the Ripley tribe (six in all) were actively engaged in the war effort, either in this country or abroad. Ruth, as already mentioned, was a nurse in the VAD moving around to various stations. Susan joined the ATS and drove all manner of vehicles from staff cars to heavy lorries. Nigel, the youngest, served with the Northamptonshire Regiment in Burma, ending up as a captain.

4

Eton Days

My days at Eton were not particularly distinguished. I ended up in the Library (a group of elected senior boys, similar to Prefects) and won my house colours. I was more renowned for my illegal exploits and as a lower boy was probably beaten by the Library more than others.

If senior boys required a 'fag' for some purpose such as sending a message to a boy in another house, or buying food in the town, they would shout, 'Boy', at the top of their voices and the last lower boy to arrive would perform the task whatever it might be. Often we would shirk the call and hide somewhere or another. If caught, and I frequently was, this meant a beating in the Library. We were also beaten for over-boisterous behaviour.

Lower boys were also allotted senior boys to 'fag' for. This involved cleaning up the study and keeping it in good order (every boy had his own study with folding bed and bureau) and cooking for the mess (two or three boys would mess together). The lower boy would provide tea, toast and probably scrambled eggs for them at tea time. They would also perform any other duties that were given to them, similar to a personal servant.

My best friend Jim Gladstone and I had many successful exploits for which we would have been severely beaten if found out. We regularly caught the bus across Dorney Common to Maidenhead to spend the afternoon at the cinema. We also went to the pictures in Peascott Street in Windsor – the street was out of bounds to us so it made entrance and exit more difficult. After careful reconnaissance we discovered a way in over a wall at the back of the cinema so we considered ourselves to be reasonably safe unless we had the bad luck to sit next to a master.

We regularly attended both Newbury and Windsor races. At the latter meeting I remember I stuck on a false moustache and Jim put on some form of disguise. As it happened on one occasion we ran into a master who knew us. Of course two boys like us stood out like a sore thumb and the master, who was a decent chap, obviously recognized us. Yet he walked past without taking any action and probably having a good chuckle to himself. In the early days our usual method of transport for longish journeys was by motorbike which we kept in a garage at Eton. Later Jim exchanged this for a car so when we became more senior we travelled in comfort.

I was a member of the Geographical Society and on one outing I lit up a cigarette at the back of the bus. The master in charge reported me on our return, rather unnecessarily I thought, and I was summoned to the headmaster for punishment. It was at a time when I had my arm in a sling, having broken a bone in a Field game house match. The headmaster, Claude Elliott, a gentle man and obviously not enjoying the task he had to perform, said as I presented my bare bottom with my head over the block, for his attentions: 'Ripley I am going to flog you gently.' It did not hurt as much as a beating with a cane in the Library although the birch, put together like a thin broom, left its mark in the shape of pieces of twig breaking the skin.

Another friend, Kim Muir, a useful gentleman rider when he left Eton (indeed there is a race at Cheltenham named after him) was also a keen falconer. We spent a lot of time together training and flying his hawks. I also kept a young tawny owl in the science rooms. It became quite tame and would fly to my hands (protected by thick gloves, I may say) for food. Eventually it escaped through a window but hung around for some days in a tall tree outside the building – though I could never entice it to come back again. There were plenty of tawny owls in the area so it would not be long before it returned to the wild properly.

By way of a little escapism during the winter months my friends and I used to hire a room on Sunday afternoons in Nell Gwyn House, Windsor, for the purpose of smoking and drinking port.

The grand occasions at Eton were always enjoyable: the Fourth of June, the Eton and Harrow match at Lords, the

Winchester match and Henley. Mother and Father would always turn up, usually with my sisters, for the Eton and Harrow match and on the Fourth of June, after a good lunch in one of the marquees, we would return to my study for tea in which a chocolate Fullers cake was a must. Particularly at the Eton and Harrow match I was very proud of walking round arm in arm with Pam, my first girl friend. Looking back, I must have been a terrible show-off since I spent most of my time walking round the Lords circuit hoping to be noticed by colleagues instead of watching the cricket. On reflection, that was about par for the course at his particular occasion.

I suppose having a cousin, Harry Birkbeck (the youngest boy to play for the first eleven against Harrow at Lords), in the same house (A.W. Whitworth's) was helpful when I first went there. Harry was a popular and unusual sort of fellow with his own circle of friends, with whom I automatically joined up, although they were slightly older. He was, and still is, an unconventional sort of fellow. You could never be sure what action he was likely to take under any circumstances. He also had a rather feudal attitude towards his fellows.

Harry had one unfortunate affliction. He was stone deaf in one ear, and the other I believe was none too efficient. As a result of this he got into a certain amount of trouble unwittingly. One evening during extra studies the House Master, Aymer Whitworth, having listened to confusing replies from Harry told him he was like a 'rudderless ship'. Harry, mishearing, thought Whitworth had called him a 'ruddy little shit'. He worked himself up into a fury and threatened to report him to the headmaster for insulting behaviour.

Everything considered, I enjoyed my days at Eton, particularly when I became more senior. The reason, I think, was because we were brought up to be individuals. The fact that every boy has his own room fosters a spirit of independence. Of course we had our team games: cricket and rowing in the summer, the Field game in the winter. This was a really good game and very much an individual effort – contrary to other forms of football we were penalized if we passed the ball. Unfortunately no other school played the Field game so we mostly played inter-house games. We also had a lower boy competition which our house usually won – the reason being that we had a bunch of big strong lower boys who failed to make it to upper school until they were getting on in years. Apart from the set games we enjoyed fives and squash which we fixed up amongst ourselves and we had plenty of time to wander around the town or push off for a walk up the Thames.

I carried on with my boxing at Eton and held my own, but I was never very good; yet I improved when I got older and stronger, boxing welterweight for the Regiment. The swimming facilities were basic and unhygienic, although we boys didn't think so at the time. Lower boys swam at Cuckoo's Weir, which was a 'cut' from the Thames, and upper boys, if they chose to, could swim in the Thames itself from the 'Acropolis', a built-up place from which we dived in. In both swimming places all sorts of flotsam and unpleasant things floated down, yet I don't remember any epidemics breaking out as a result of these conditions. Nowadays they have a fine new swimming pool both indoor and outdoor, close to the school.

In the athletics field I was again fairly undistinguished, with two exceptions. I enjoyed cross-country runs and seemed to be able to stay on quite well, usually finishing in the first bunch. I carried on with this activity when stationed at Old Bolingbroke before going abroad. Our company commander, Donald Hamilton, was a great enthusiast and keep-fit fanatic. He would frequently summon officers in their rest periods and at short notice for a long run. Indeed he once chivvied us all out after our Christmas dinner. My main athletic achievement was the high jump; as a lower boy I was about the best in the school and was usually a contender for a prize when I became a senior.

There were some extraordinary and eccentric beaks at Eton in my day, none more so than the two Marsden brothers, 'Horse', a housemaster, and 'Bloody Bill'. The latter was a very tall gangling man with legs that appeared to come up to his arm pits. He was a brilliant mathematician although intimidating with his gruff ways. When the lesson had finished he would invariably end up with blackboard chalk all over his clothes. He would sometimes lie in an ungainly way on his desk and quite unconsciously draw lines on his posterior – much to the amusement of his pupils.

Two little incidents illustrate Bloody Bill's unpredictable personality. Out for a walk one March day, Horse Marsden, after taking a deep breath, was heard to say to his brother, 'Spring in the air.'

Bloody Bill replied, 'Spring in the air yourself!'

During the summer months Bill spent a lot of his time coaching fours or eights on the Thames. He would bicycle on a rough tow path with his megaphone, issuing instructions. Once he became so carried away that, quite oblivious to his whereabouts, he bicycled straight into the Thames.

'Oily Pete' Channon, another maths master, on retirement came to live in Bucknell, the next door village to us in Shropshire. He was particularly remembered for his caustic and lavatorial comments in class. Once having farted quite loudly at his desk, he looked up and said, 'Pardon me gentlemen. Queenie and me had hot buns for tea.' On another occasion when a boy let out a loud fart in class, Oily Pete leapt up from his desk and, pointing an accusing finger, said 'Boy, bet that browned your pants!'

One day Channon evidently became fed up with his pupils farting in the classroom and ticked them off as follows, 'You horrible little boys you sock in Rowlands (the tuck shop) then come in here and rumble in your pants.'

The Rev Mr Beasley, a housemaster, was a most flamboyant man of the cloth. All Etonians of my vintage will remember him driving at great speed and a lot of noise through Eton in his 'Yellow Peril'. This was a fine old type, sports Vauxhall painted bright yellow.

'Knickers' Nickson, my classical Tutor, was a particular friend and help to me. He had an attractive little house close to Barnes Bridge which I used to visit two or three times a week for extra studies. Once we had settled down in comfortable armchairs he would offer me a cigarette from a silver cigarette box. I found this form of tuition most relaxing and rewarding.

'Jelly' Churchill was another famous character, indeed an institution to us rather dim lower boys who found ourselves in what was termed the 'Army Class'. He was a very kindly old fellow and incredibly patient; his nickname derived from the fact that his lips resembled jelly when he talked. Churchill was a distinguished looking man and I should not be the slightest bit surprised if Sir Winston was related to him.

Aymer Whitworth, my housemaster, and his wife, Alice, (incidentally a relation of my mother's) were a delightful couple. Very much of the old school and they ran a good house. To us boys, though, housemasters' wives never seemed to have much to do with things. It was the 'Dame' who we came in contact with and was responsible for everything in the House from meals to medicine.

Mid-way during my time at Eton, Aymer Whitworth retired and he was replaced by Colonel John and Lady Rosemary Hills. The Colonel was a brilliant historian and correspondent of *The Times*. He had a very military and severe look about him and not surprisingly commanded the OTC. Much later on he became Headmaster of Bradfield. I never really got to know him very well, yet we were all charmed by his wife Rosemary. Every few years, Geoffrey Jameson arranged a dinner for Lady Rosemary and the boys who were there at the time in memory of John Hills.

5

Diana The Huntress

At eighteen when I left Eton, I suppose I could have been described as good looking, with dark hair, height about six feet, fairly slight, but well proportioned. At an early age, particularly at school in the boxing ring, I had learnt the art of self defence. There is a saying that it's the man that makes the clothes: I think I looked clean, comfortable and at home in anything I wore, whether it was a formal occasion or, later, in battle dress up in the front line.

Although I was said to have an aristocratic look about me, I had a disarming smile and a kindly nature. I was undoubtedly vain – yet a wicked glint in my eye was never far away. Fortunately I had a strong streak of determination, although I seldom took the most difficult route, not being too bothered with trivia or detail. Some people called me lucky – in fact good fortune seemed to come to my rescue in most things I attempted. I was never likely to be a real Captain of Industry, a professional man, or an academic in any sense. I left what I termed the First Division to those who considered they had the ability to succeed. I settled early on to be Captain of the Second Eleven and have a more enjoyable life and, with luck, get paid for it. Yet I always retained a kind of ambition and felt devoutly that nothing was impossible. I was always attracted by the words of the American musical, 'Anything you can do, I can do better'!

I remember one occasion about this time when Diana's parents gave a dance in their country house in rural Herefordshire. I was considered a suitable escort for Ann, who was blonde, rich, and rather sexy. We were driven to the dance by a chauffeur in the old Daimler. Although rather inexperienced I felt we should not waste a good opportunity since we were alone together in the back of the car. It was a cold evening and we had been provided with a fur rug to keep out the elements. Ann, more experienced in situations of this sort, snuggled up and her leg became entwined with mine. We kissed. I decided to take a risk and slipped my hand down the cleavage of her dress. This was exciting. Her breasts were firm and responded to the touch. Although I was fearful of receiving a slap on the face at any moment, Ann was evidently enjoying herself and instead of drawing back she moved over and lay across her escort.

Mindful of the Ripley family motto '*Dum Spiro Spero*' ('While I breathe I hope') I eased myself into a comfortable position and began to get to work. At that moment the tyres crunched on the gravel of the short drive and we came to a stop outside the front door. A hasty repair job was necessary and we joined a throng of guests being ushered into their respective cloakrooms. I had already lost a button and had a vivid smear of lipstick on my collar. That was the last I saw of Ann.

A restorative in the shape of a strong drink was now called for so I moved into the bar and cooled off not without a ribbing from some of the my friends who suggested that a polite guest sometimes departed with lipstick on his shirt but never arrived in that way. Enjoying my second or third strong snort by the window sill adjacent to the bar my attention was drawn to a stunning figure in a red dress. She was tall, long brown hair, high cheek bones with a sort of Mongolian look. She looked like a good looking boy dressed up as a girl, with a small chest and shapely limbs.

She caught my eye and held my gaze, as much as to say, 'Why don't you come over and ask me for a dance.' I ambled over and said to her, 'Hello, I am sure I have seen you before somewhere. What's your name?'

'Diana,' she replied, 'I am the girl they are giving the dance for; but I have seen you – at least a view of your backside at the point to point last Saturday. I was at the jump where your horse ran out and you disappeared, apparently out of control towards the river.'

I remarked: 'Well we seem to have something in common – at least an interest in racing and a sense of humour.'

'As a matter of interest what happened to you?'

'The brute wouldn't stop so I aimed him at a good deep pool

in the river. He came to a sudden halt on the bank and I toppled in. I was retrieved by a keen fisherman, who was not best pleased because I had spoilt what he considered to be a promising bit of water. Have a dance?'

We danced every dance together except a Paul Jones but I managed to cut in successfully and restore the *status quo*. Over supper, I learnt that Diana was a good horsewoman, enjoyed shooting and fishing and we made a date to meet next day. From then on we met two or three times a week. I was astonished at her prowess at all country pursuits. One autumn afternoon we decided to wander around after a pigeon. Diana was armed with her 'pea-shooter', a 410 shot gun, me with my 12 bore. Out of the blue two duck came over very high. I fired with no result. Nonchalantly, Diana, with a graceful movement, eased her little gun up to her shoulder and fired. The two ducks came hurtling down both stone dead.

It was the same fishing in the border country brooks such as the Teme, the Clun and the Arrow. Diana invariably landed her fair share of the basket. Distances were unimportant in our expeditions; sometimes we would bicycle twenty miles to the meeting place. Other times we would ride horses and when petrol became short I took out a pony and trap.

The river Clun always had a fascination for me. When I was very small I toddled off after a picnic party and disappeared down the rapids. My godfather was fishing below when he felt a bump against his waders. On looking down he saw this little brat swirling down under the water. The godfather leant down, retrieved the child and brought it to dry land. After I had been held upside down for a few minutes I revived and toddled off again, evidently none the worse for the experience.

On another occasion a few years later I was after a rising trout in an awkward place under a tree. In order to get into a better position to present the fly to the fish I balanced myself on a low-lying branch of an elder tree. The branch collapsed and I disappeared into a swirling pool. At that particular spot there was a strand of barbed wire, presumably to keep out cattle when the river was low. I struck out and a sharp barb went through my cheek. So there I was impaled by the head just above the water. Fortunately, my brother Derek, fishing upstream about a hundred yards away, heard my plaintive cries, came running down, grasped the predicament, splashed into the water and unhooked our poor hero. I have a scar to this day to prove that fishing can be a dangerous pastime.

Then again in the hunting field, if you can call it that, Diana and I would go many miles to meet up with the rough border country pack of hounds.

The excitement and thrill of seeing each other was everything. Sex didn't come into it. Yet we were both aware that there was a strong physical attraction. Now it was time to carve out some sort of career, but Diana was never forgotten.

6

Office Boy

In those days a father would do everything possible to launch his sons on careers he considered to be most suitable for them. He would do this by approaching relations, friends and acquaintances and would go to great lengths to ensure that the boy got a good start in life. In my case it was decided that I should go for business; so through some strings pulled with distant relations, I entered a firm of East Indian merchants at their head office in Glasgow.

The purpose of this experience was for me to become a tea planter in Ceylon. First I had to gain experience in office routine, the ultimate task being to write up the vast company cash book. The training period generally took about two years. The various departments were equipped in a Dickensian manner: high desks and very high stools. It was the custom generally to stand up to work at the desk which was found to be very tiring for the first week or so; but individuals became used to it and at least there was no chance of going to sleep.

The routine for new arrivals was basic office boy work in the postal department. I did up parcels containing samples of piece-goods for customers in the Far East. I also relieved the telephone operator, a particularly difficult task for an Englishman. The Glasgow accent at the best of times is difficult to understand but when accentuated over telephone wires I inevitably distorted messages. I proceeded round the various departments until one day I was told to report to the Cash Department. This was real progress and provided I didn't make a hash of my time there I could look forward to a posting out to the Far East in about a year's time.

The first drama occurred when I was sent off to collect £400 cash from the Royal Bank. This I did as requested, but having forgotten to take along with me the usual briefcase in which to deposit the money I stuffed the notes into my pockets. In the street on the way back to the office I ran into a pal who suggested we should have a cup of coffee together; we began talking and decided to drop into the local hostelry for a pint. Two hours elapsed – it usually took five minutes to perform this task – and the cashier was becoming understandably very concerned about his cash. Telephone calls were made, messengers were sent out and indeed the police were informed. Returning from my very agreeable outing I reported to the cashier and emptied my pockets on the desk. The money was correct, but the cashier was much shaken thinking I had either absconded or been abducted. I received a severe rebuke.

Some months after this incident I had an evening appointment for a game of tennis. The time was drawing on and try as I might I could not get the cash book to balance. This was a huge book with countless numbers of columns which recorded all transactions for the day and it had to be written up every day for the Auditor's inspection the following morning. There seemed to be no alternative: if I was to play my game of tennis with my friends, I would have to cook the book. I discovered a most ingenious way of doing this and on the face of it the cash book was balanced for the day.

Next morning Mr Sloane, the Auditor, came in as usual and the cash book was placed in front of him on the high desk immediately opposite mine. This job usually took Sloane about ten minutes and he left having certified the book as correct. On the morning in question Mr Sloane had been studying the cash book for a full forty minutes with a very puzzled expression. Meanwhile I was getting on with my work and trying to ignore both Mr Sloane and Mr White, the cashier, who was at the high desk on his left.

Mr White was a most frightening man. He was aged about sixty, never laughed, wore square-toed boots and had a perpetual drip at the end of his nose. Mr White could sense that there was something wrong and transfixed me with a very nasty look whenever our eyes met. After another excruciating twenty minutes Mr Sloane asked Mr White to come over to his side of the desk to look at the cash book. He stumped round casting a most hostile look at me. The error had been found. I, of course, had been perfectly aware what the trouble was all along.

Mr White, after a minute's discussion with Mr Sloane, beckoned me over to the other side of the desk. Looking most severe he pointed to an entry in the vast book and said in a very broad Ayrshire accent, 'What's the meaning of this?'

I replied, 'I am so sorry, Mr White, I thought it went into that column.'

Pointing a threatening finger at me Mr White finished the awkward situation by saying, 'Ye no' paid to think in this office, laddie.' He did indeed have a kind streak and I was even known to get a smile out of him on rare occasions.

Fishing trips at weekends and summer evenings with my friend Dick, with whom I shared digs, were my main pleasure in those days, and there were few lochs or rivers within fifty miles of Glasgow that we did not take fish from either legally or illegally. One weekend we set off on Dick's motorcycle and side-car to the Trossachs where we heard there was good trout fishing to be had on Loch Catrine. The trouble was that the fishing was reserved exclusively for residents of a nearby large and splendid hotel. In spite of having no money we booked in and enjoyed an excellent day's fishing, landing quite a nice bag of trout. In the middle of a very good dinner the harsh reality dawned upon us that a stiff bill would be presented next morning. We decided to touch the head waiter, who was a kindly old fellow, and on hearing our story he was happy to oblige and slipped back twenty-five pounds. It was a bill which was repaid, with a grateful letter of thanks, when we were in funds again.

One Sunday morning we decided to go up to Loch Lomond by bus with our trout fishing rods. We passed a river which appealed to us so we got out and cautiously reconnoitred the water. To my surprise I saw a lovely salmon break the surface in a most accessible place. In no time the rods were up and this fine fish was hooked. None the less I was apprehensive on three counts. First and most important the monster fish might break me or get off, since I was fishing with only a tiny trout rod; secondly, there was a fair chance of detection, being close to the road and presumably on private water. Thirdly, salmon fishing is illegal in Scotland on Sundays. My luck held. The fish became tired and Dick went into the water and scooped it out. Fortunately I had a poacher's pocket in my tweed coat, but even with the collar up, the tail flapped around my neck. The bus journey back was anxious to say the least and rather unpleasant for the fellow passengers because the fish began to pong in the warm temperature.

Midway through my apprenticeship my father rented a farm house in Argyllshire with good sea trout fishing and rough shooting. The whole family, six children in all, turned up together with our relations and friends including my girl friend Diana. It was a very successful and enjoyable holiday, notwithstanding the weather. The rain pelted down continuously day and night. Being a spate river these conditions were just what was wanted and there was a good run of sea trout and the occasional salmon. The farmhouse was always in a ghastly mess, the place being littered with wet clothing and muddy gum boots. It was a holiday in which the family and guests lived entirely off the land. The menus consisted of grouse, duck, pigeon, rabbits and a plentiful supply of fresh fish, augmented by the farmer's potatoes.

In true 'sexist' fashion it was the girls' duty to prepare the food, cook it, and wash up. My contribution towards the food supply was not up to my usual high standard, and it was often remarked upon. The reason for this, needless to say, was the presence of Diana. My sporting instincts were blunted. We were inseparable and our fishing took second place. Returning to Glasgow in my old banger with Diana at the end of the holiday, I decided to impress her and lay on a slap-up dinner in Glasgow's best restaurant. We had drinks in the cocktail bar and a fine repast. I was as proud as punch escorting this very pretty girl in the Mal Maison and all eyes were upon us, including one of the directors of my firm who gave me rather a suspicious look knowing that my salary would not go very far towards the bill.

Inevitably the bill arrived and was paid, but it was a near-run thing. After emptying all wallets, pockets and purses we were one shilling to the good which was given to the head waiter. He accepted it with dignity, courtliness and thanks in the true tradition of this famous establishment. Indeed he wished us every happiness. Many years later I was to return to Mal Maison in a rather different role.

7

The Pearl of the Orient

A second-class berth had been booked for me on a large P & O Liner sailing from Liverpool to Colombo in what was then still called Ceylon – 'the Pearl of the Orient'. Having said goodbye to my parents at the dock I went aboard with my dog Pestilence, a huge animal half foxhound and half lurcher.

A kennel was specially made for Pestilence, which remained on deck throughout the voyage. The dog and his master had a very enjoyable time aboard – the latter particularly because he met a number of interesting people through his dog, who became a great favourite with his fellow travellers.

One particular friend called Betty was a fairly young – ten years older than me – divorcee, rich and a first-class passenger. She took me under her wing and evidently fancied me. Through her I spent most of the voyage in the first-class part of the ship and was looked after in a very agreeable fashion. This was just as well because my total wealth was ten pounds, given to me by my father on departure at Liverpool. I was rather disgusted at his paltry hand-out to a son who was being shipped to the Far East on a five year stint. I was told that I would receive a remittance from time to time when I arrived at my destination, but I was so incensed at this frugal treatment that I decided there and then that I would paddle my own canoe in the future and would not accept any further payment from my father.

And I never did. On reflection later on I decided that my old man, who was such a likeable and endearing person, thought he was being generous. Although owning thousands of acres of land Father was a truly impoverished landowner who never had any cash. In those days the rents he received from tenants in no way covered the cost of repairs and maintenance to keep the property in reasonable order. He, in common with many others at that time, suffered from a horrifying bank overdraft. His estate was left to him entailed so he was unable to sell anything to redeem the situation.

Betty considered herself an expert on fortune telling through palm reading. Always sceptical about these things, I allowed her to practise her gift on me. Midway through the session she went quite white and started to tremble and would not continue. I was not unduly concerned about this but nevertheless I was curious, so I ordered a glass of brandy on tick from the bar and asked her to explain why she was so distressed. She took my hand again and explained that my lifeline came to an abrupt stop at an early age which, in palmistry terms, meant that I was going to be in mortal danger within the next few years and the chances were that I would die. Maybe this was a portent of future events, yet I dismissed this incident as a lot of bunkum.

My only previous experience in this field was when I had a day's outing as a schoolboy to Henley Regatta. There were many sideshows at this event including the Wall of Death, fat women, the notorious Rector of Stiffkey in a Barrel (the Rev Harold Davidson, later eaten by a lion at Skegness) and a fortune teller. I entered the soothsayer's tent where an evil looking old hag was gazing into a crystal ball. Amongst other things the old witch told me that I would be having an exam soon and that I would pass. This suited by book very well. I did no more work for the rest of the term and failed.

The other person I got to know quite well aboard was an attractive female cabaret artiste who did a turn every evening with her troupe. I was to meet her again at the Gall Face Hotel in Colombo.

The estate tea lorry was despatched to Colombo Docks to pick me up together with my tin trunk and (unbeknown to my future boss) a large dog and a kennel. Pestilence happily jumped into the back of the lorry where there were remains of soggy green tea leaves. I was in front with the driver, a Sinhalese, who wore a shirt and white sarong and no shoes. There was no communication, because neither knew the other's language. It was an agreeable journey and I was struck by the beauty of the place. Sometimes we went through minor jungle areas, but mostly there were little settlements of

Sinhalese mud houses with colourful locals wandering around. The girls were attractive with long black hair, some coffee coloured, others darker. They were aware of their attraction and had a challenging, come hither, look. They wore a white or pink bodice, then a gap of flesh round the midriff with a long coloured skirt which was tucked in around their hips.

After we had been travelling for about thirty miles the road petered out and we came to a wide and deep river. The driver manoeuvred the lorry on to the estate ferry, quite a small craft which only took one vehicle at a time. The ferry was hauled across the river by a series of ropes and ended up at a primitive landing stage on the other side. This was the only access and when the river was in flood during the monsoon, the Halwatura Tea and Rubber Estate was totally isolated.

We arrived at the *Perrier Dori's* ('Big Master's') bungalow, situated on the top of a hill with tea bushes all around. It was a pretty setting with a large expanse of lawn in front of the house, reminiscent of an English garden, but there the likeness ended. The house and garden were covered with a profusion of blooms from bougainvillaea and hibiscus to morning glory and other exotic tropical shrubs. Jack, the boss, dressed in a white shirt, white ducks and a pith helmet, was awaiting us on the lawn. I got out and shook hands while the driver undid the tail board of the tea lorry. Immediately Pestilence leapt out and rushed towards Jack, jumping up and covering the boss's smart white clothes with green gunge from the back of the lorry. This was not a propitious start, particularly as I knew I would be spending two or three months as a guest at the bungalow until I learnt the ropes and had a smattering of the language. The next day being Saturday, Jack was due to go to Colombo for a day's racing followed by a Ball at the Gall Face Hotel. He asked me if I would like to come along.

And so we set off in his smart chauffeur-driven car with evening kit for the party. We split up during the day and only met at the hotel ready for the festivities. I had a thoroughly good time, but at the appointed hour of departure back to the estate could not be found, so Jack was driven home by himself. In fact I had found my cabaret girl friend that I had met on the ship coming out. The troupe was giving a show at the Ball. We were delighted to see each other again and at her suggestion I went up to her room and spent the night with her.

Since my day clothes had been taken back to the estate in Jack's car, I had no alternative but to appear for breakfast in my tuxedo. This caused a few raised eyebrows amongst the hotel guests, many of whom were planting friends of Jack's. Indeed an item appeared in the gossip column of the *Colombo News* the next day, telling the story of a very new young planter's exploits at the Ball. About mid-morning, after a few reviving Horse's Necks, I was most relieved to find Jack's chauffeur at the door ready to take me home. I thought that I was in for real trouble when I got back to the estate. Would I be shipped back to England? There were 'blacks' all the way along the line and there was nothing as yet to commend me.

Surprisingly I received a splendid welcome back at the bungalow, and Jack's Australian wife was equally pleased to see me, having heard of my adventures. It was difficult to know what sort of age Jack was. He was probably about fifty. He had certainly fought in the 1914-1918 War with distinction and collected some medals. It was known in Glasgow that he was a pretty tough customer. He had been planting in Ceylon for about thirty years and was much respected as an honest and honourable man and a good disciplinarian – after all he had achieved the rank of Adjutant of the Highland Light Infantry (sometimes called the Glasgow Highlanders) whilst serving in His Majesty's forces. Yet after all the years in the tropics it was thought he may have gone a bit bush.

Jack was about five feet ten inches tall, weighing around fourteen stones. He had a gruff voice and was well muscled for his age on the top half, with quite a belly below. He enjoyed the good things of life and was undoubtedly successful in running one of the most profitable tea and rubber estates which the Company owned. He also had a very nasty temper and had in his time floored members of his labour force who seemed to him to be truculent.

So it was with some fear and trepidation that I returned to base. His first words were, 'Glad to see you back. Pestilence has become a great friend and we have given him a good dinner.' Intrigued by my activities the previous night, he added, 'I hope it was all worthwhile.' I replied that it was, and recounted some of the details – not all, because I was reluctant to divulge everything in the presence of his wife.

Unbeknown to me, Young, the Boss in Colombo, had

telephoned to Jack and told him about the evening's exploits, having enjoyed a few Horse's Necks with me at the Gall Face. Whether this was the reason why I received the all-clear was never resolved. I thought not. Jack, after so many years on his estate, was beguiled by this newcomer. The episode reminded him of his youth and he decided to give me the benefit of the doubt – inwardly thinking, no doubt, 'We've got a right one here.'

I was sent round each day with a native overseer to learn how things ticked on the estate, and to pick up as much of the language as I could. I went through the whole programme – planting the young tea bushes, cultivation, pruning, plucking, weighing the tea and factory work (that is converting the green leaf into drinkable and saleable tea); paying the labour force once a week and supervising rubber tapping and production.

Most of the labour force were Tamil, originally from South India, but many were born in Ceylon. It was important therefore that I learnt to speak Tamil as number one priority. The rest of the labour force were composed of Sinhalese, an attractive race but inclined to be indolent. There were small Sinhalese villages dotted around the estate and the men and women were employed as rubber tappers, or given contracts for weeding areas of tea. This helped to eke out their modest standard of living which was derived from coconuts, palm trees, from which they made toddy and arrack; a few semi-neglected rubber trees, and the inevitable emancipated looking cow, which was practically part of the family. Yet they seemed content and happy people.

Drinks were brought out on the lawn regularly at six pm. The usual tipple was a bottle of Dewar's White Label with soda and ice. The boy announced that dinner was ready when the bottle was empty. Jack had been somewhat displeased with me for the first few week's stay at the bungalow because I had insisted on a gin and tonic for the evening session. The reason for this was that my father, at the time of his ten pound tip at Liverpool, had warned me of the perils of life in the tropics and issued some instructions to me. They were as follows: 1) Don't get into debt; 2) Don't consort with the native women; 3) Don't drink whisky; 4) Remember the sun is your enemy not your friend.

The last instruction was sensible advice. I always wore a

pork-pie hat with a banana leaf stuffed inside. The older generation wore the conventional topée; but always a hat. Of the other points, gin and tonic was soon discarded in favour of whisky. Although the additive was known as 'Indian Tonic' it was heavily laced with quinine and had a most unpleasant taste and it was quite impossible to consume any quantity of it.

Jack was pleased at his success in weaning me on to the spirit of Scotland and thereafter we consumed many bottles together. He was also amused at the fatherly advice I had been given, but did touch on the remaining two points. While agreeing on the advice about getting into debt, he conceded that I would inevitably have difficulty in that department – particularly if I had frequent outings to Colombo. He explained that everything was done on the 'chit' system, whether on the estate or in Colombo. The '*Chitti*', or money-lender, had his shop by the factory, and was always happy to advance money plus interest to interested parties against a chit – repayable at a negotiated period of time. The *Chitti* was a very rich man. He owned the tea lorries, and was responsible for transporting the finished product and rubber to the docks in Colombo, as well as collecting the green tea from various parts of the estate and delivering it to the factory.

On the remaining point ('Don't consort with the native women') Jack was most emphatic – though by this time the Australian mistress had returned to the Antipodes for a few months' rest, so we were able to talk freely. He reminded me that the Tamils constituted a large majority of the labour force, about half of them being women, and they were all very good workers. Indeed, if it were not for the Tamils, who lived in what were known as 'coolie lines', it would be impossible to run the estate. Jack's summing up was succinct. 'I don't mind what you do when you get to your own bungalow, but don't work them day and night.' This seemed to be a clear indication to keep off the Tamil element of the labour force.

8

A Planter's Life

The time had arrived for me to go off on my own. I had reached the stage when I would be known as 'Sini Dori' (small master) and have the responsibility of running a large area of tea and rubber. My own bungalow was about two miles away from Jack's, along twisting estate roads through tea and rubber plantations. It was attractively situated on a hill with a wide verandah all around, a nice lawn, and pretty tropical trees and bushes. The tea plantation, with its acacia shade trees, surrounded the garden. The bungalow consisted of three bedrooms, a dining room and lounge together with primitive bathrooms and loos. The latter was known as the 'thunder box'. When the chain was pulled a load of earth was deposited into a moveable septic tank below – it made a noise like thunder.

I resolved early on that I would install proper plumbing in the place. I acquired text books on the subject and drew a plan. In fact it turned out to be a much more complicated operation than I had anticipated. The gradient had to be right and the angle of the bends had to be worked out carefully. There was an unholy mess for several weeks but the estate masons, who had never done this sort of work before, made a magnificent job of it and everything worked perfectly. The only problem was burying the cost. Being out on a limb I had a budget for my division under many different headings – for example, pruning, plucking, cultivation, roads, coolie lines and clearing jungle. I succeeded, quite unbeknown to Jack, in salting it away under the general heading of cultivation.

I was spurred on to this hygienic activity by the possibility of Diana coming out. A trip to Australia had been arranged for her with friends and the idea was for her to come and stay in

Ceylon for two or three weeks on the way back and on her own. I felt that the thunder box would not be very conducive to romance and happiness during the proposed stay.

The servants' quarters, an L-shaped elongation, were at the back of the bungalow. In those days planters never visited the kitchen quarters. It was never expected that they should do so and indeed it would have been resented, for this was the domain of the 'Boy'. This Boy was a most likeable middle-aged Tamil who spoke English and Sinhalese. He was a good cook and kept the place clean and tidy. He had been in service for Doris all his life and was helped in his kitchen domain by a '*podium*F' – a Tamil youth. Whether the Boy kept a wife or wives in his quarters I never discovered because I simply never visited that area.

Where there is food in the tropics there are usually beetles, mice and rats and where there are rats there are very often snakes. Perhaps this was the reason why planters, over the years, had been discouraged from visiting the kitchen in their own bungalows.

In order to move around my tea and rubber division – about two thousand acres of cultivation – I needed a vehicle. I was not given one on the firm so, with the help of the *Chitti*, I bought a very ancient Fiat and also a motorbike.

Every morning, except Sundays, I was woken up by the Boy at five thirty am with a cup of tea so that I could appear at 'Muster' at six am. All the labour force assembled at this hour – if they were late they were fined or sent home without pay. There I would allocate work through my *kanganis* (foreman) and they went off to their various duties. So far as I was concerned it was no hardship getting up early. It was nearly light, pleasantly cool and I soon became accustomed to this way of life. The Tamil labour force had to rise much earlier and it was necessary for them to have a good meal of rice and bits and pieces before they set out for a long day's work and the women had to prepare something for the family to eat at midday. At least they went to bed early and there was never any sign of a light in the coolie lines after eight or nine pm.

After Muster, I returned to my bungalow for a substantial cooked breakfast. The appetite was keen after an early rise and it was still comparatively cool. At about nine am I would set off on my rounds usually on foot with my two dogs, Pestilence and

Misery (a Kangaroo hound which I acquired soon after my arrival). My standard dress was an open neck wool shirt (to mop up the sweat), khaki shorts, stockings and desert boots and of course the pork-pie hat with a banana leaf stuffed inside. I always carried a home-made walking stick to help me on my way and it often proved to be a useful weapon if snakes were encountered. I would check on the number of trees the pruners had dealt with and if they had done the job badly fine them and send them back to their lines. On one occasion my pruning budget had become overspent so I dictated through my *kangani* that each pruner would have to clean prune seventy bushes instead of the usual fifty. This was a very skilled job and extremely hard work. The men glistened with sweat. As a result of this edict the pruner's went on strike.

This was a situation that had not occurred before and I was rather concerned about it but I stuck to my guns and had the support of Jack. After a week on strike they returned to work and finished their allotted tasks of pruning seventy trees by midday. It was later confirmed that there were some Communist elements at work at that time, with incidents of hijacking tea lorries *en route* to Colombo. Fortunately there was no further trouble and, although new at the job, I achieved the status of a tough boss and gained the respect of the whole labour force.

Continuing my tour around the estate, I would probably head for the pluckers. It was always a pretty sight to see a line of thirty to forty girls with colourful sarees tossing the green tea leaves into baskets hanging down their backs and suspended by a bit of cord from their heads. This was quite a regimental operation. The women were kept in line by the overseers and went down the rows of tea and woebetide anyone who missed out a tea bush. Furthermore, the tea bush had to be left as flat as a table. If they plucked the *arambu* (the young leaf not properly formed) or failed to discard any old shoots which were not acceptable at the factory, they were in trouble – probably fined and sent home. Yet they filled their baskets with harvestable green leaves with great dexterity using both hands.

It was a source of amazement to me how they carried out this strenuous task for nine hours a day, often walking a mile or two from their lines to the allotted starting point. But this was their life. They had been trained to it from a very early age and seemed to be perfectly happy. I tended to be a little partisan when visiting this scene of operations. From the labour relations point of view I felt I should join the pluckers and either encourage them or tick them off. On most occasions my eye was attracted by a lissom young Tamil who was perfectly aware she was about to be approached. With the heavy weight of the tea basket her bosoms escaped from the saree.

Then I would try to converse in the lingo, perhaps mildly reprimanding her for incorrect plucking but taking no further action. We would part with a smile and she would get on with her work. These encounters were useful for me, both for *espirt de corps* and for getting better acquainted with the language. On the other hand if I had the misfortune to walk up a row of tea which was badly plucked (not as level as a table top) I would summon the *kangani* and tell the woman to report back to him. If, as sometimes happened, she was an arrogant, gnarled old hag she would be sent home and fined immediately.

At midday and at four o'clock in the afternoon the pluckers assembled at he predestined meeting place on an estate road where the tea lorry would be waiting. This was known as the 'weigh-in'. The baskets were weighed and the number of pounds collected by each woman was recorded. They received money for the fruits of their work on Friday's pay day. I felt it was necessary to check up on these weigh-ins from time to time. It was sometimes found that jiggery-pockery went on, either through relationships or the attractions of a pretty plucker.

By about eleven am the sun was really hot and even Pestilence and Misery were beginning to tire of hunting mongoose or hares. This was the time of day that I moved off to supervise the rubber tapping – at least there was some shade. Sinhalese men and women were employed as tappers. The bark of the tree was cut at a slope with an implement resembling a chisel. Each new cut produced latex which dripped down into a receptacle which was invariably a half-coconut shell. The shells were emptied every afternoon into buckets, collected by estate lorries and delivered to the factory. It was the overseer's job to ensure that the tapper did not cut into the tree itself when shaving the outer skin for the production of latex. If this happened the tree was wounded, and after a few months lumps would appear. This was serious and could never be corrected. After about a year the outside skin would regrow and that panel would be retapped. If lumps had appeared in the interval production would fall and indeed the tree itself would be of little use thereafter.

Once I detected a row of rubber trees which had been very badly tapped. There were wounds on all of them. After a lot of searching around the extensive rubber plantation I found the culprit and took him along to show him the damaged trees. The tapper, a truculent type of Sinhalese, which was unusual, said in so many words, 'So what'. This attitude made me see red. I called up the dogs who made a show of attacking him (little did the tapper know they never would). He was cornered so I moved in with a solid right to the chin. He was laid out cold. The news went round that the new *Sini Dori* would not tolerate insubordination and shoddy work. The tappers work improved after that.

Away from the shade of the rubber trees, I would walk back a mile or two with the dogs through blocks of tea to my bungalow. By noon it was really hot and I was relieved to sit down on a wicker chair on the verandah, dripping pools of sweat and drinking a pint or two of cool passion fruit juice which the Boy had learnt to produce immediately on my arrival. I would then have a shower, put on a sarong, and have a good lunch (sometimes known as tiffin). Next came siesta time. Planters were fortunate in this respect; during the searing heat of the afternoon they always had a kip – different from their colleagues in Colombo, 'office wallahs' dressed up in suits and ties. A planter on a visit to Colombo with his bronzed, weather-beaten, and healthy appearance could always be detected straightaway from the flabby, pasty-faced office wallah.

In the afternoon I rose from my bed about three thirty pm, checked up on the various operations and attended the evening muster and the tea weigh-in. Sometimes I would go to my little office to do the books – but not often because it was uncomfortably hot and the place was swarming with Borer beetles. These flying insects, about three times the size of a bumble bee, made a fearsome buzzing noise and had a dangerous sting. They bored into the woodwork of the little office.

On returning to my bungalow I consumed more soft drinks, wrote letters or read, had dinner and retired under my mosquito net in bed at nine or ten pm. I never drank hard liquor on my own and, strangely, the thought never occurred to me. On the rare occasions when I had visitors or Jack turned up, it was quite a different matter and the bottles of Dewar White Label were produced.

This, then, was an average day's work apart from Friday, pay day, when the whole labour force, numbering some hundreds, assembled. I sat at a trestle table with piles of rupees in all denominations around me. The names were read out together with the amount due. For the first few times this was quite a daunting experience because the whole operation was conducted in Tamil. Having no English people to talk to, I picked up the lingo quite quickly and was soon to pass an oral exam, conducted by the visiting agent, which entitled me to extra pay.

Besides the normal production of tea and rubber I had quite a large budget for contract work. This was spent on building and repairing coolie lines, making new estate road and culverts, weeding the tea plantations, clearing jungle which surrounded the estate on three sides, or clearing a block of old unproductive rubber trees for replanting. When clearing operations were in hand the contractor brought in elephants to do the work. It was fascinating to watch them. First the coolie would hack away at the earth surrounding the tree, severing some of the branch roots, then an elephant would be brought in with a *mahout* astride the front end of the beast, armed with an evil-looking pole with a nasty spike at the end. This implement was used to goad the beast in order to get it to do the job in hand. The elephant was then directed head on at the tree where it would literally use its weight and push the tree down. Often the tree would only come so far down, being still secured by the tap root. Then a well trained elephant in a most nimble way placed his two front feet on the sloping trunk of the tree and applied its weight. The tree came crashing down and at the same time the elephant nipped off the tree like a cat. The branches were immediately hacked off by a gang of coolies and other elephants hauled the timber up to an estate road.

The *mahout* and his elephant had a great affinity and understanding towards each other; yet if it was goaded too far, or it may have been in 'must', the elephant might dislodge its mahout and trample him to death. This was probably a marginally better fate than occurred on one occasion with a particularly irate elephant. The beast, having dislodged its keeper, caught hold of him by its trunk and smashed the poor fellow against the nearest tree.

Bribery and corruption was rife. When tenders were put out for a contract, the *Sini Dori* had many applicants bearing gifts. Fortunately for the firm, I think that I was an honest and fair man and I would never accept a bribe. I was offered money, gems, cases of whisky, but I never succumbed to the temptation – in later years I rather regretted this; I might have put by a nice little nest egg. There was no doubt that the English and Scottish community of planters were by and large honourable men and they set a fine example in preserving their own sphere of honesty and integrity.

When I made a deal with a contractor I was very happy and pleased to receive a basket of fruit grown locally – and nothing else. There had been times when a weeding contract was negotiated with a local Sinhalese villager who had pretty, nubile, daughters. This might help to clinch the deal, and possibly turn the routine day's work into something more exciting.

Early on, after being despatched to my own bungalow, I decided to confide in my own Boy who, after all, had a wealth of experience in attending to the whims and foibles of lonely and sometimes sex-starved planters. I asked the Boy what he thought would be the best method to adopt, indicating that I was keen to learn Sinhalese because I would receive a higher rate of pay if I succeeded in passing the exam in this language, being now quite conversant in Tamil. The Boy, an old hand at this game, fully understood my dilemma and volunteered to go off to Kandy to procure a young, attractive and good caste Sinhalese young lady. He was away for about three days, while I stayed with a fellow planter.

On returning to the bungalow I was greeted by the Boy, who was all smiles. He had probably had a good time himself and reported that he had been successful and brought the girl back with him on a bus together with her few belongings. Where she was hidden for the next few months I never did discover, the Boy feeling that it would not be prudent for us to be seen together in the daytime. At about nine pm that evening, having retired early yet expectant, I heard a rustling on the verandah outside my bedroom and observed two ghostly figures. The one quite tall and the other very small. This was it. The Boy introduced Sophie and withdrew to his own quarters. After some initial embarrassment, I invited Sophie into my bedroom. There was just a dim light and, not knowing any Sinhalese as yet, sign language had to be resorted to. She followed me to the bed and although very timid, appeared to be willing to please and took off her colourful sari. This was quite a simple and speedy operation and there was no delay for the removal of bra and knickers; she was not wearing any.

Now I had an opportunity to observe the girl – child would probably be a more correct description. She was about five feet tall, very pretty, quite light-skinned with long black hair down to her waist. Yet she was very young. Her little breasts, only recently formed, poked out and her pubic hairs were hardly discernible. It was evident to me that I was the first man she had ever slept with. She was short of technique but a ready learner and instinct dictated to her the right moves. I decided to treat her with kid gloves for the first meeting. I caressed her, and although apprehensive, she responded with a warm and loving embrace. I later discovered from the Boy that he would only produce for his master's pleasure a high caste virgin from up country. Puberty occurs early in the tropics and girls, barely out of childhood, marry at an early age.

Sophie mysteriously appeared every evening, sometimes I would be in bed before she turned up; on other occasions she would be there under the sheet possibly asleep. She usually disappeared about five am before it got light, as mysteriously as she arrived.

I found that this method of learning the language – known as a 'sleeping dictionary' – was most successful. We came to know each other very well and enjoyed a remarkable rapport. Indeed she had a good sense of humour. Of course there were drawbacks. In order to make herself, in her eyes, more attractive and sexy, she covered herself with a cheap and sickly-smelling powder. I did not have the nerve to dissuade her from doing this; after all, she was trying to please.

After some months it seemed to me that Sophie was becoming rather overfond of me and tending to be possessive, even indicating that she might take up residence and meet my friends in the daytime. This was quite taboo. If the situation had gone as far as that I would be considered to have 'gone bush' and, even in that outpost, news travelled quickly. I would be ostracized by the white population for living with a native. On the other hand, night operations conducted with diplomacy were considered to be perfectly permissible. I concluded the time had come for Sophie's departure. She had been a splendid nocturnal companion and I had become fairly fluent in Sinhalese. Besides this I had made the acquaintance of other dusky maidens who lived locally. So there was a tearful parting when I gave her a few simple gifts and a wad of rupees. The Boy escorted her back to Kandy.

My predecessor had dammed up a large stream which flowed through the far end of the estate, and a fine swimming pool was the result. With the labour force I erected a diving board and constructed in the manner of the native houses a two room bathing hut. This was a splendid set-up and much admired by visitors. The temperature of the water was perfect and I found a swim in the evening after a hard day's work in the tropical heat to be most refreshing. The only thing missing was some local talent to go swimming with – and perhaps some relaxation afterwards. I engineered this to perfection. Two sisters, Rosie and Salome, had become occasional visitors to the bungalow after the dismissal of Sophie. It was, after all, necessary for me to continue to get to grips with the Sinhalese language! These two girls, together with their mother (herself by no means unattractive), were, at their own suggestion, installed in an isolated house on the edge of the jungle on the other side of the stream opposite the bathing hut.

At this time I had organized (on tick) an old Riley racing car with a history. In its time it had been a regular competitor at the Brooklands circuit with Freddie Dixon at the wheel. It had no doors as such, merely a cut-away place each side to step into; no windscreen, twin open exhausts from the engine to the rear end – and it made an almighty noise.

On evening visits to the pool the girls opposite would be alerted some minutes before my arrival, and were usually splashing around in the water very scantily clad. It did not take too long to encourage them to disrobe beforehand and thereby keep their clothes dry. The girls enjoyed fooling around in the water and could swim well enough, propelling themselves along with a natural dog-paddle action. After the swim I would select one of the girls and spend an agreeable half an hour in the bathing hut. There was never any question of jealousy. Sometimes if the two sisters were away the mother would swim over and present herself for the master's pleasure.

Although the estate was remote and inaccessible, my planter friends were keen to pay a visit at a weekend. After a game of golf on a short course around the rubber trees with the aforementioned stream as the boundary – all, needless to say, constructed by the labour force – guests would repair to the bathing pool to cool down and enjoy the company of the nubile girls. If guests stayed the night at my bungalow there was rarely little trouble in producing some home comfort, if they were that way inclined; they usually were.

If the 'regulars' were unavailable, the Boy was despatched to the neighbouring village to put the word around that the *Sini Dori* required company. More often than not Bertha would turn out. She was practically white, tall and of fairly large proportions. Her father was a planter of yesteryear and no doubt the villagers selected her as the most suitable person to please the young master or his guests. In fact she proved rather disappointing and uninterested once on the couch, and had been known to pick off pieces of crumbling paint from the dilapidated walls at moments when she should have been thinking of other things. In retrospect I sometimes think that I might well have received a knife in my back for the way I carried on. Yet no thought of this nature ever occurred to me at the time. I was an employer to some of them, and a friend of them all, and for some intangible reason I gained much respect. It was probably because I would, having an enquiring mind, always stop and talk to anyone who was around and discuss ordinary things, in their lingo, such as their own family life, the names of their children and so forth. I might talk about the jungle, which was just alongside, to discover if it was worth rising extra early to have a shot at a wild pig.

Other periods of recreation were spent with Jack, the *Perrier Dori*. For example on Sunday mornings in the wet season we would go off together to shoot snipe in the local paddy fields. It was mostly walking up, but sometimes we would hire about a dozen boys and have a few drives. The bag was usually about fifteen to twenty snipe. There was a long-standing custom that if any of the locals were hit during the shoot they would receive one rupee per pellet. On more than one occasion it had been known that a line of old women had been placed along the *bund* at the end of the paddy field and when shooting began they would come over the top in the hope of receiving the odd pellet and the customary reward. The snipe would set off, jinking around and keeping very low, making a difficult target and the old grandmas were astute enough to lie low when the guns got close to them.

After these snipe-shooting expeditions we would return to Jack's bungalow and have a late breakfast, followed by a few snorts which usually took the form of a Horse's Neck. Then a big Ceylon curry lunch was the order of the day. The Boy and his assistant would come along with plate after plate, sometimes as many as a dozen spicy ingredients, which were added to the mountain of rice. A good kip was essential afterwards.

Some evenings Jack would come up to my bungalow for a drink. We mostly reminisced about times in England or Scotland and Jack would leave when the bottle of Dewar was finished. There was always a perpetual din of crickets and frogs croaking, whilst overhead the spectacular and rather eerie sight of the large flying foxes was entertaining. The whisky was consumed rapidly with a large amount of soda per tot. It is necessary to drink a considerable amount of liquid in the tropics; when we had finished our drinking session we were usually wet through with sweat, our trousers sticking to the seat of the chairs.

Sometimes by way of recreation I would stay with a friend up country to play in a rugger match. I played wing three-quarter for KV, the local club. In those days you stuck to the wing and went straight for the corner flag, having sucked two or three glucose tablets before the game. The pitches they played on bore little resemblance to Twickenham, being bone dry; most players ended up scarred and bleeding.

At other times I would go off for a weekend with my friend Charles to the dry zone jungle near Hambantota, which was proper big game country. On more than one occasion they had a race to the South Eastern Province, me having the legs on the flat in my racing Riley, while Charles went away up the hills in his hotted-up Ford. The driving was done at night and the real danger was encountering a wild elephant or buffalo. Some near misses occurred. These large beasts never hurried when crossing the road and should one or other of us have collided with the animal it would most likely have been curtains at the speed we were going.

On one trip to Hambantota Charles took his wife Pat, and I took along with me my new servant, a useless sort of individual who was scared stiff of the jungle and spent most of his time locked up in an old saloon car which I then had. Charles and I planned an early morning big game safari yet we were a little disturbed about Pat while we were away, so we decided upon a bolthole for her up a tree in case there were any marauding beasts around. The three of us spent a cosy night in the tiny tent and well before dawn the two hunters set off. We moved on steadily, well into the heart of the jungle along game tracks, breaking off twigs every two or three hundred yards so that we could identify our route back to our camp. As dawn broke there was a stirring in the jungle. There was a chatter of monkeys, scary shrieks close at hand of parakeets and jungle fowl, grunts of wild pigs, and the trumpeting of an elephant not all that far away. We proceeded with caution having come face to face with a buffalo just emerging from a waterhole. Fortunately it ambled off. Buffalo are dangerous and unpredictable beasts and will charge for no reason at all.

The next unusual sight was a dead python, fully twenty feet long and as thick as a man's thigh. There was little flesh left, the vultures having evidently found it the previous evening and had a good meal. Following some pig up a dry river bed, we heard an unfamiliar crashing noise all around us. We stood stock still, scarcely breathing, until the herd of feeding wild elephants moved on. A herd of elephants is comparatively harmless unless you get in its way. The danger is the lone elephant, a rogue, that may be carrying some lead and could be suffering from festering sores – they seek vengeance and charge without provocation. Charles, an acknowledged hunter, had been called upon on a number of occasions to deal with one of these beasts. Having been kicked out by the herd they raid the villagers' settlements and one elephant can do untold damage to their crops besides scaring the daylights out of the villagers themselves. A shot through the ear with a heavy 4.5 elephant gun is the solution, but skill and a good nerve are required.

The next encounter was with a leopard, again a dangerous

and unpredictable animal. As we proceeded along the dried-up river bed we heard a noise as if someone was sawing a tree. We moved on cautiously with rifles at the ready and after covering a few paces the beast leapt out of the undergrowth and disappeared into the bush – not affording us a shot. As hunters tend to do we pushed on further into the jungle in the hope of meeting up with a bear; there were known to be some around the area. We were oblivious to time in the excitement of the safari until one of us looked at a watch and found out it was ten am – the time at which we were supposed to have returned to camp. We tried to retrace out steps in the hope that we would find the broken twigs to get us back on to the right route. We found no marks whatsoever and in spite of following numerous false trails and covering many miles we had to accept that we were lost. By this time it was becoming very hot and the thought of survival was beginning to enter our heads. Suddenly Charles let out a yell. He had detected a broken twig. The excitement and relief were intense. Sure enough, we soon found another, and another which led us back to our clearing.

We were presented with a strange sight. Pat was right up at the very top of the bolthole tree and complaining bitterly. It transpired that some buffalo had appeared at about eight am so she had shot up a tree to escape. She sat in the fork of the tree until the beasts had pushed off and was about to come down when to her horror she saw a bear below and furthermore it was starting to climb the tree. In total panic she went on up the tree as far as she could go. The bear wandered off after a time, but Pat remained stuck in the topmost branches, quite unable to get down again. She had been up for about four hours and, when rescued, was not best pleased with the two hunters for not returning on time. Of course we never confessed we had been lost.

Back on the estate, work went on as usual, interrupted by various dramas amongst the labour force. I was now considered to be capable of sorting out any troubles or fights which arose on the coolie lines. On many occasions a bleeding male or female would be brought up to my bungalow with a deputation of coolies arguing as to the cause of the beating up. I listened carefully to their stories and, as expected by them, in my capacity as both judge and jury I would pronounce judgement and severely fine the guilty party. On one occasion I detected that a large ruffian, and a known trouble-maker, who had been up in front of me before had badly beaten up a girl. He was an arrogant sort of individual, a bullying type who accused others of the assault.

Knowing that he was lying I decided to teach him a lesson. In a rage I gathered my stout walking stick and went after the culprit. After a long chase through tea and rubber plantations, with Pestilence and Misery giving tongue, I caught up with the rogue and really set about him. I left the unfortunate fellow in a sorry state; but the labour force were satisfied with this form of summary justice and there was no further trouble in the lines for many months.

A few days later I had a murder and a suicide on my hands. On an outlying part of the estate a coolie reported a freshly dug mound of earth from which a nauseating smell exuded. A digging party was set to work and a decomposed body was unearthed. Now the matter was in the hands of the police and in due course I had to give evidence. It transpired that the deceased was quite a well-to-do fellow and that he had been murdered for his possessions.

The suicide was a sad and pathetic incident. I was called to the scene of the tragedy where I saw a young fellow, whom I knew as a good and honest worker, with a rope round his neck, hanging from a shade tree in a tea plantation. Although the police were called in there was no great fuss about this and it turned out that the poor chap had been jilted in love.

* * *

The day had now arrived for me to be tested on my knowledge of Tamil and Sinhalese. I knew that the visiting agent was not much of a linguist, but in order to safeguard myself I put the word round to the labour force that the exam was imminent with a severe warning that if anyone failed to understand me, should they be chosen to talk, they would be sacked immediately and would be expelled from the estate. They responded magnificently and I passed the exams with flying colours.

Sinhalese was a complete walk-over because I detected early on that the visiting agent had practically no knowledge of the language at all. I was told to talk to some toothless old hag who was messing around her house and ask her why she was not working. I asked the question but understood not one word of the response. I merely made up a plausible story that all the others members of the family were out working; that she had been sick all night and too weak to work that day. The visiting agent was well satisfied and congratulated me on having such a good knowledge of both Tamil and Sinhalese.

Knowing that Ceylon has its full quota of venomous snakes, scorpions and other unpleasant reptiles, a resident in the country parts soon develops a sixth sense of the dangers that are lurking about. For example, it was unwise to walk around the bungalow, whether in the rooms or along the verandah, without a light, and slippers should always be worn. It was vital to have a good look into one's shoes before one put them on. I once had a narrow escape when I found a scorpion in my walking shoes which were placed a few yards from my bed. The creature was rapidly despatched.

Jack once had a very close encounter with death. He was setting off from his bungalow to the office when he felt some sort of movement in his topée. He removed the hat and gave it a tap but there was apparently nothing there. The hat was replaced and he walked on. Again he felt a movement so the topée was taken off and this time he gave it a good bash. To his horror a krite, probably the most deadly snake in the East, fell out. It is a small snake and had evidently found a comfortable resting place in the head-band.

One day I entered my living room after a morning's work and found a large snake curled up in my favourite chair. Once alerted, the reptile, about ten feet long, rushed around the room like a demented thing, moving at great speed with me in hot pursuit. I was quite aware that it was merely a rat snake and quite harmless. It got away.

Cobras were a different kettle of fish; not only are they deadly poisonous, but they put up a good fight when cornered. They coil themselves up, but the head and about a yard of snake rears up in a most menacing manner. A hood appears over the already expanded head of the cobra and it makes an evil hissing noise. Its forked tongue darts out and it strikes. It is as well to keep your distance at this stage. I had accounted for many of these reptiles. The secret was to use a fairly long walking stick and whack its neck when it reared up, thereby breaking the backbone and immobilizing the snake. It could then be despatched without too much trouble. The cobra cannot jump and can only strike from the position it gets itself into.

From time to time cobras around the bungalow were a nuisance, when they were attracted by the smell of food and probably rats in the kitchen area. The cook and boy became hysterical and my services had to be called upon. These incidents usually happened when it was dark and it was sometimes difficult to deal with the snake when it holed up under the verandah with its head poking out and making a vicious noise. A shot gun was the solution in such cases.

There was only one King Cobra I left alone and indeed it scared me. I was travelling around an estate road on my motorbike when I spotted the snake on the side of the road. I parked the bike and went to investigate, thinking the snake would slither off into the tea bushes which they usually did unless they were cornered. This cobra, a huge thing, advanced and continued to advance towards me, rearing up in the accustomed way every few yards. The snake had crossed the road and seemed intent on pinning me against a high bank on the other side. Deciding that discretion was the better part of valour, I moved smartly towards my motorbike and sped off. From then on I decided to treat the cobra with rather more respect that I had hitherto.

Jimima, as nicknamed by me, was a charming little Sinhalese fellow aged about ten. He joined the household staff to feed the dogs and to look after any other pets that were acquired from time to time. His other duties were to take my shoes and socks off and produce slippers when I returned, sweating and exhausted, from my morning rounds and also to provide jugs of cold orange and passion fruit juice to restore me.

Besides Pestilence and Misery, I kept a pet monkey, a Siamese cat and a leveret. A strange thing happened with the young hare. It was kept in a spare unfurnished room where it was given food and water and became quite tame. One day when Jimima and I paid a visit, the room was empty and the hare had disappeared, yet there was no way it could have escaped. On closer investigation it was found that the door was not quite flush with the floor and there was a little gap but this was not big enough for the hare to get through. The only possible solution was that a rat snake had got into the room, killed the hare, swallowed it and squirmed out again through the gap under the door.

* * *

News at last arrived by letter that Diana, now on an extended trip to Australia with friends, would be calling in to Colombo on her way home in about a month's time and would leave her party and stay at my bungalow for a few weeks. The excitement and preparations were intense. Trips to Colombo were made to buy new curtains and covers for chairs. The bungalow was given a complete spring clean and the staff were as excited as their master at this forthcoming event. Everything was in apple pie order for her arrival. Yet there was a threatening cloud on the horizon. Rumours of a possible war against Germany were rife and, although reporting in Ceylon papers on news at home was rather sketchy, the outlook looked ominous. In fact I and the other planters in our isolated existence did not bother ourselves much about the situation and felt that the matter would be sorted out satisfactorily in due course. The possibility of a war was ruled out altogether.

One day, returning from my trek around the estate, I was greeted by an anxious-looking boy holding a telegram. It announced that Diana's ship would be calling in at Colombo shortly, but her guardian had decided that she was to continue the voyage home directly due to the uncertain world situation and the threat of war. This was a shattering blow for me after all the build-up and excitement. I called the guardian every name in the book and considered that he was quite unjustified in coming to this decision. I passed the days in a very unhappy state of mind until the date of the arrival of the ship in Colombo harbour. At least this was better than nothing; my spirits rose. The old racing Riley was tuned up and made as spick and span as possible by the factory mechanic. I set off in fine style, crossed the Kala Ganga on the ferry, and roared off, making a tremendous noise, and duly arrived at the docks.

I found Diana immediately amongst a welcoming crowd of people and we had a very happy reunion. She looked stunning and it was a very proud moment for me. There was no time to be lost, however, because the captain had decided to return home at a good speed and with a minimum amount of delay. Instead of a day in the harbour, a mere three-hour stop was scheduled, enough for revictualling and taking passengers on and off. Immediately Diana and I set off in the car for a brief tour around the countryside. In spite of considerable discomfort (she sat on the floorboards) she enjoyed the trip and was beguiled by the way of life of the local inhabitants and amazed at the greenery and colour of the country. We returned to the Gall Face Hotel for lunch but the time was nearly up.

I took her back to the ship and went aboard. After a look around, a visit to her cabin, and some refreshments there was a sad farewell. Neither of us knew what the future had in store. I decided that the best thing to do was to drown my sorrows so I sloped off to the Grand Oriental Hotel and did precisely that. About midnight, tired, and rather unsteady on my feet, I decided to set off in the car back to the estate. I have a hazy recollection of the early part of the journey; evidently I had been travelling fast with the purpose of keeping awake with a rush of air in my face. It was to no avail. I dozed off. The car hit a culvert, crashed into a rubber tree and somersaulted back on to the road again, upside down and still moving. I was impaled, with my head outside, bleeding profusely.

My life was probably saved by the cut-away door. I remained in this undignified position for some time, making weak cries for help until some villager arrived on the scene who lifted up the side of the car allowing me to escape. I then spent the remainder of the night on a coconut couch in a village hut. The next day I hitched a lift back to the estate on a tea lorry and that was the last I ever saw of the dear old Riley.

9

Call To Arms

When news finally came through that war had been declared I was told to report immediately to my unit, the Ceylon Planters Rifle Corps, in Colombo. For the next few weeks we were busy erecting defences on the seaward side of the city and engaged in patrols and sentry duty – and having a fine old time in the evenings when we were not on duty.

Once the rudimentary defences had been completed the unit was told to stand down and the planters were ordered to return to their estates and produce as much tea as possible as shortages were anticipated. Later on most of my fellow planters found themselves in Burma. I was keen to get back home and join the British Army. My father came to the rescue and arranged for me to join the Coldstream Guards once I got back.

Now there was a certain amount of last-minute clearing up to be done: handing-over, disposal of dogs and other pets to friends and so on. But the matter which gave me more concern than anything else was to leave the country with all debts paid. I had been living on tick for the last two years so this presented quite a problem.

A meeting with my creditors in Colombo was duly set up. These consisted of tailors, shirt makers, stores and hotels. I explained that I had no money, only a few possessions and a car (by this time a fairly ancient Standard saloon) and a motorbike. A man from Cargills, a smart store, acted as spokesman for the creditors. I suggested that I should hand over the car and motorbike in full settlement for all bills and that I required a signed statement that I was released from all my debts. The creditors were perfectly happy with this arrangement and the deal was struck. They probably did quite well; certainly no cars were imported into Ceylon for the next five years.

I duly set sail in a P & O liner which was rather empty. The voyage, so far as the passengers were concerned, was uneventful but tricky for the Captain. The ship was unescorted so the order for the day was 'full steam ahead', making sure she kept well off the usual shipping route. The Mediterranean at this stage of the war was comparatively safe, but once past Gibraltar and out into the Atlantic it was quite possible to be detected by enemy submarines. The Captain took a zig-zag course and made many detours. At one stage it was acknowledged that the ship was nearer America than England. These problems did not bother the passengers too much. The bars were open, the food was good and I had a comfortable cabin. Indeed there was dancing aboard under black-out conditions.

There was one rather attractive dark haired girl aboard by the name of Joan, an Anglicized White Russian. I did not take too long to strike up a friendly relationship with her. We danced, looked out to sea under the moon and the stars, and a real ship's romance got under way. Many promises were made for the future once we arrived home, but in spite of a trial it didn't work.

At least whilst aboard I managed to read all of Tolstoy's *War and Peace*.

* * *

Before joining up I had a good time in Shropshire during the 'phoney war' period when life seemed to go on much the same as usual apart from coupons for food and petrol. The latter restriction curtailed my visits to Diana to some extent until I hit on the idea of using a pony and trap, which was a most refreshing and enjoyable form of transport. Diana was as attractive as ever and spent most of her time 'digging for victory' in the family's large walled garden. However she did seem a trifle aloof and a little preoccupied by something or other. I was suspicious that she might have become entangled with the RAF who were stationed nearby.

One day I took a train to London to meet friends and to find out how the war had affected the Metropolis. Nearing the outskirts of London, the train crawled along and finally stopped. On looking out of the window the whole of the city seemed to be lit up. Flames shot up and one could hear muffled explosions. This turned out to be the first German raid on the Docks. The driver eased the train slowly into Paddington Station where I found a taxi and proceeded towards the West End. I booked into the Cumberland Hotel, Marble Arch, which was comparatively deserted. I was given a comfortable room at the top of the building where I was one of the very few occupants. The other guests had transferred to the ground floor and many of them were huddled under stairs and in other nooks and crannies. The noise of anti-aircraft fire was deafening with a blast every now and then; but some distance away.

I stayed in London for four or five days and each evening the bombing intensified. The City and East End were receiving the brunt of the attack with quite a number of bombs dropping in the West End. The evening before I returned to the country I toured around visiting some old familiar haunts. As I headed for the Cafe de Paris, an 'in' night-club in those days, there was a pall of smoke around the premises and a fleet of ambulances lined up. To my horror a succession of stretchers were being carried out. Only a few minutes before a bomb had fallen through the glass dome of the building and exploded on the dance floor which was packed. There were many casualties, quite a high proportion of them being Servicemen and women.

I was awaiting my call-up papers to join the Coldstream Guards but nothing happened so I decided to enroll with the King's Shropshire Light Infantry, the local county regiment, where my brother Edward was a regular soldier and commanding a Depot. A week after I joined up as a private, the survivors from Dunkirk began to arrive. They were a most dishevelled and undisciplined lot. Once they had all turned up the Commanding Officer ordered them to form up on the parade ground. He then proceeded to lay into them, saying that he had never seen such a shower in his life. He told them that they were not heroes but part of a defeated Army. They were to draw new uniforms and arms from the Quartermaster and were threatened with the Guard Room if there was any breach of discipline. In this way order and morale were restored.

I was next selected to go to an Officer Cadets Training Unit, in my case Sandhurst. I blotted my copybook right from the start by arriving late. My old sports car had broken down and I failed to get up the following morning to draw my rifle. I was a marked man from then on and received a lot of stick from the ferocious Guards Company Sergeant-Major and Staff Sergeants. In spite of the unpropitious start, I enjoyed this tough training programme and after six months passed out and became a 2nd Lieutenant in the KSLI.

The only incident worth relating was at a dinner in the hall when, as a promising cadet, I was seated at the top table on the right of the Adjutant, Eddie Goulbourne. The port had come round and I, in a nervous state, downed it in one. I was rebuked by Goulbourne who told me that not only had I consumed the glass of port before the Loyal Toast, but before he himself had touched his. Strangely he was rather entertained by this incident and the last I saw of him was riding a white charger up the steps of the old building after the final passing-out parade.

Back at the Depot, I soon adjusted myself to a junior officer's life. I had no responsibilities and was still being trained. One evening I took out an Auxiliary Transport Services girl for a pub crawl in my old car. We called on many hostelries and at a late hour the car broke down and was abandoned. The next day the girl and I went to retrieve the car but there was no sign of it. It transpired that it had been collected by the police and put in their pound alongside the county police station and it was believed there were some charges impending. This was bad news because I had just been ordered to report straight away to the 1st Battalion in Lincolnshire. I hatched a plot, with accomplices, to recapture the car under cover of darkness. This proved to be entirely successful and I duly reported to my CO in Lincolnshire on time. I subsequently learned that the police were quite baffled about the 'case of the missing car'.

I now had to undergo some strenuous training as a Platoon Commander with my men. They were a tough and suspicious lot, a high proportion of them being Welsh coal miners. They were slow to accept someone new, but once through the barrier they proved a grand bunch of fellows. For a month my troops and I were allocated the agreeable job of potato picking. The men were given extra pay and got their feet nicely under the table at the various farms. I did even better. I merely visited them once a week with their pay packets and spent most of my time hunting with the Belvoir on a borrowed horse.

The girls in these parts were found to be most accommodating and their numbers were swelled by an influx of WRAAFS; there were many airfields in the area. I experienced one rather embarrassing time after an all-ranks dance at Ludham. I took Elaine, a WRAAF, out to a nearby hayfield for a tumble and afterwards we fell asleep in a somewhat uncompromising position, waking up in broad daylight in full view of the village and the troops' billeting area. We beat a hasty and bashful retreat much to the amusement of the onlookers.

A trip in a three tonner was arranged at least once a week to Norwich. This was the troops' favourite place. The pubs did a roaring business and there was no shortage of female companions. Indeed I struck up a regular relationship with a good-natured girl whom I met each Wednesday at nine pm under a wall in the city.

On one very hot summer day I found myself giving a lecture on some military topic to a company of soldiers in a large Nissen hut. I knew my subject well and had a bundle of notes to guide me if necessary, but in the middle of my rather boring lecture my attention was drawn to a window where I could see a leaf being blown about in the breeze. My mind switched off completely; my only thought was of that leaf which evoked lovely summer days in the country. I remained in this state for some minutes much to the embarrassment of my audience. It was no use. I had lost my thread and was practically unaware of where I was and what I was doing. I dismissed the class. This episode proved to be a useful and salutary lesson, for later on I was called upon to give many lectures and to make many speeches.

The Battalion, now fully equipped and mobilized, next found itself in Scotland. It moved around from Blairgowrie, then Inveraray, finally to Callender, an attractive small town in West Perthshire with a very good hotel. It was here that I met a young Scots lass who was seeing the New Year in and who was eventually to become my wife.

The River Teith runs through the town and it was also here that a six pound anti-tank gun came off its pulleys during a river crossing exercise and disappeared. It is probably still there. At this stage I was in command of the Anti-Tank Platoon and a further disaster, or near disaster, was shortly to befall me.

I was in charge of a Brigade Firing Practice exercise at the seaside with live ammunition. The idea was to hit a target which was towed along about two hundred yards behind a tracked vehicle, thus simulating a moving tank. All went well until one idle gun team laid on the carrier (towing vehicle) and fired. It was a direct hit and the carrier was written off. Luckily the driver leapt out unscathed. Fortunately before a full blown inquiry could get under way, the Battalion moved to Greenock and boarded the *Empire Pride* for service overseas. Officers and troops were fit, highly trained, and eager for action. Once at sea they learnt that their destination was Bone in Algeria where they were to join the 1st Army. Once again I was travelling the seas unescorted, but this time the situation was more serious because a battalion, together with vehicles, was aboard and German submarines were becoming more active.

On the second night at sea, I was the officer on duty and amongst other things my duty was to check the 'look outs', whether they were below decks or anti-submarine men. In all I booked six soldiers for sleeping or being inattentive. This was a serious charge and a court martial was promulgated aboard the following day. They were all found guilty. This had the effect of tightening up discipline and getting the troops to realize that there was serious business ahead. There was an uneventful landing at Bone, livened up a little by an enemy aircraft being shot down nearby. The troops marched a long way with full kit and eventually dug in to a reserve position along the front line. The general plan was for the 8th Army, now under Montgomery, and the 1st Army (my outfit), commanded by 'Sheep' Anderson, to meet up on the Mediterranean coast with the intention of destroying or capturing the German/Italian enemy.

Apart from minor skirmishes my battalion was engaged in two or three major battles to capture the mountains overlooking the plains of Tunis. This was the real indoctrination of war and the troops stood up to the task well. Fortunately there was negligible aircraft activity but serious shelling and mortar fire and tanks appeared from time to time but not in reach of my gunners.

I remember practically kicking away mortar bombs that fell around, including 'Nebelweffers', a new and nasty device with six to eight bombs at a time. I was still new to the job and did not bother too much about my own safety. My men, together with the six-pounder guns, were usually left well in the rear – not through orders or my own fault but because the towing vehicles, called 'Lloyd' carriers, became stuck in the mud and their tracks came off. But I managed to encourage a gun crew to manhandle one of my 'pieces' to a forward position from which an enemy machine gun post was holding up operations. A hit was registered and the Battalion advanced. That may have been the reason for my being mentioned in despatches in this area.

The 1st Army captured the mountains and advanced along the plains, only to be held up when they came to Tebourba which was not very far from the coast. My guns at this stage were pulled by 'carriers', tracked vehicles but more reliable then the 'Lloyd'. My leading carrier crossed the river at a ford but when proceeding along a sandy track on the other side it was blown literally sky high. I ended up on my backside, dazed, but quite unharmed, gazing at the river. It was clear that this sandy track, the only exit, was dotted with 'Teller Mines' – some completely hidden from sight.

The Teller mine was about the size of a large soup plate, three to four inches deep, with a primer and a heavy explosive charge. Since there were no Sappers around I took it upon myself to defuse the mines. This was done by gently unscrewing the primer and throwing it away and thereby rendering the mine harmless. The Germans had a nasty habit of booby trapping some of the mines they laid in such a way that when unscrewing the primer the mine blew up. Fortunately for me, I was unaware of this practice and I was successful in making a route through for my trapped vehicles.

A few days before this incident, when attacking Hill 101, I was ordered to get many guns up with the leading troops in case of a surprise attack by tanks over the brow. The hill was given a good blasting by our Artillery and mortars and there was thick smoke and a smell of cordite everywhere. Germans were expected to be encountered at any moment. Passing a dug-out in my carrier, a black face emerged with a greeting and some abuse. He turned out to be an old school friend in the Scots Guards, George Mann of the brewing family who later captained England at cricket as his father had done before him. Mann's company had previously captured the hill but had lost all communications with Headquarters. He and his men had suffered a heavy bombardment from our own side. George received a DSO for the part he played in this engagement.

The only other incident which I clearly remember before the complete surrender of the German/Italian armies at Hammamet, just outside Tunis, was when I was acting intelligence officer at Battalion Headquarters after the Hill 101 encounter. Signals coming through were few, so the officer decided to have a kip with a telephone at his elbow. But I could not get off to sleep; whichever way I turned I started to itch. There was a stream nearby so the next morning I went to clean my teeth and have a wash. On opening my shirt fully, insects began to leap out. I was infested with fleas – evidently the Battalion HQ tent had been pitched over a recently evacuated Arab Nomad encampment. A comparative lull in engagements followed so I despatched my man to the rear to collect a new shirt and shorts. The old clothes were discarded; there was no way to get rid of the fleas. They had penetrated every crevice of the garments and water seemed to have no effect on them.

It was most rewarding to see thousands upon thousands of the defeated enemy when the two Armies met. They looked a bedraggled and motley lot, mostly Italians who never did have very much stomach for fighting. The greater part of the élite German Army had been evacuated. The next two or three months were spent in a tented camp near Hammamet on the edge of the Mediterranean close to Tunis. At that time it was still very French and the Frogs seemed to resent the influx of British troops. Yet there were some civilized places about.

I did not receive the full benefit of this rest because I was allotted various tasks. My first job was to take a trainload of prisoners together with tracked vehicles on 'flats' to Algiers. This was a long journey on a very slow train and the trip lasted three or four days. I took over one of the flats and lived on it for the entire journey. Rations were handed out from time to time and I augmented the diet with eggs and chickens bought from the Arabs along the track. This food was cooked on the open flat while the train was making its slow progress. Many minor fires had to be dealt with.

The Arabs were expert at stealing. One night I lost all my clothes, except those I was sleeping in and my boots. The thieves had no trouble in climbing aboard the slow moving train and leaping off again with their booty. I managed to scrounge another pair of boots and enough clothes to make myself presentable by the time we pulled into Algiers. The prisoners were duly paraded and marched off to a prison camp. I and my friends from the train now had a few days leave in Algiers. It was a magnificent city and all the more so because it had been quite untouched by the war. It was then the seat of General Eisenhower and his Headquarters.

There was a famous night spot known as the Sphinx away up a hill in the Arab quarter. In fact it was a very plush and superior brothel catering for Europeans only. Once in the place one was greeted by girls of all nationalities; there were bars, bedrooms, and a non-stop 'exhibition'. A number of very high ranking officers were usually to be seen at this establishment. One evening my friends and I, after making merry at the bar, secured ringside seats for the exhibition. Two girls were making love to each other. One of them had a false penis attached to the front of her body and was going through the full copulatory action. At the height of their excitement I leant over and grasped the elastic which supported the dildo; I pulled it as hard as I could and then let it go. There was a resounding smack and the girl leapt up rubbing her buttocks and hurling invective in French at me and my pals. The management were alerted and my party was unceremoniously slung out. Yet I was to visit the place again unchallenged and I managed to behave myself more in the manner to which they were accustomed.

Returning to my Battalion I found that I had to go to Enfidaville, some miles down the coast, so I hitched a lift from a New Zealander flying a Lancaster cargo aircraft. He had a co-pilot and I was the only passenger. Making myself as comfortable as possible in the enormous hull of the aeroplane, I dozed off, only to be awoken by a severe jolt on the head. The aeroplane had suddenly dropped a thousand feet or more and was put down on a small landing strip. I could not see out but sensed there was something seriously wrong. There were a series of bumps and jars until the aeroplane eventually came to rest. Once out I was surprised to find that the plane had settled down in a thicket, well off the runway. The pilot, after making sure I was OK, was quite unconcerned and merely said that he had run out of petrol and decided to come down at the first place he could find.

Instead of enjoying myself on the beaches of the Mediterranean with agreeable visits to Tunis, I was again despatched for other duties. This time it was a rock climbing and mountaineering course in the Atlas mountains. I did well and enjoyed it so much so that I was retained, becoming a divisional instructor in rock-climbing. Soon the Battalion was moved up to the foothills of the mountains and everyone was put through a course under my organization and supervision. There were many hair-raising experiences. Officers or other ranks who seemed to show aptitude were selected as leaders or anchormen. They went up first driving pitons into the sheer rock face to which ropes were attached, making sure that the tip end of the ropes were securely belayed.

The troops came up, some of them scared out of their wits because of the height and sheer drop below. It was found that a few soldiers, whatever encouragement they received, were quite unable to cope and were thus a danger to their colleagues. They genuinely suffered from vertigo. Rumours were rife as to the reasons for this mountain training, and there was much speculation as to our next assignment. I remained in the Atlas mountains, training other Battalions in the Division until my metabolism dictated that I had had enough and I went down with jaundice. I recovered at a field hospital at Château Dame on a strict diet augmented by surreptitious and quite unsuitable hard-boiled eggs purchased from little Arab boys, who crept under the flaps of the big marquee. Once released from hospital, I was put on a train to rejoin my colleagues who were stationed in the Tunis area. There was a lot of drink aboard this train so, with some newly acquired friends, I decided to celebrate. On arrival I was very ill indeed and had to spend a week in bed. I felt I was going to die, and probably would have if I had not been young and fit. Drink and jaundice, it seems, don't go together.

Once more I and my platoon were sent off, this time to Carthage to dig air-raid trenches and defend the perimeter of the house where the big three, Churchill, Roosevelt and Stalin, had an Allied meeting. They were most elaborate air raid dug outs and tailor made for each individual. There was much ribaldry about Stalin's bolt hole. In the event they were never used, and security was so tight that I and my men never caught sight of these wartime leaders.

Sure enough, the troops' intelligence network proved to be well founded. The Division was to attack and capture the fortress-island of Pantilleria as a prelude to the Sicily landing. This was a combined Navy, Army and Air Force affair with a heavy pattern of bombing by the Americans immediately before the assault. Heavy casualties were anticipated and indeed the place looked virtually impregnable as the troops went ashore from landing craft. In the event it turned out to be a more or less bloodless victory. There were a few scattered shots from the enemy, then a sea of white flags. The Germans had been evacuated and the positions were held by Italians who felt that self preservation was better than fighting.

I had a most interesting role in this engagement. Once my guns were ashore I was ordered to capture the C-in-C, an Italian Admiral, in his palatial subterranean hideaway and take him to Division headquarters. I selected six stout men, all sergeants, and well-armed. We duly entered the place and found that practically everything worth having had been destroyed. My batman discovered a nice Olivetti typewriter in good working order which was smuggled out, but they had to be careful of the nasty little 'Red Devils' – anti-personnel devices which were scattered around all over the place. I and my sergeants went on to the end of the tunnel and entered a pleasantly furnished room. There at a desk sat the Admiral in full dress, looking as smart as could be.

I approached the desk and saluted him. He stood up and returned the compliment. Then we both sat down and I was offered a cigarette. I took it and we both lit up. I then explained the purpose of my visit, telling the old sailor that his troops had been overrun and that I had been ordered to take him to Headquarters. The Admiral stood up, unbuckled his dress sword and handed it to me, saying that he was happy to surrender. That sword, together with a few Luger pistols I had collected, remained as one of my prize possessions until it was stolen sometime during the Italian mainland campaign. The six sergeants took the prisoner away to Headquarters after a farewell salute and that was the last I saw of the Admiral.

It was not anticipated that the Battalion, still practically unscathed, should return to the African mainland so soon. Nothing very much happened there apart from training, swimming from the Tunisian sandy beaches, and evening frolics in Tunis. By now a mutual respect had grown up between me and my men. Leadership is difficult to define. Some officers relied on stern discipline, often without any charismatic touch or feeling. My attitude was always 'to ride them on a loose rein' with the idea that the rein could be tightened up in tricky situations – thus keeping something in reserve.

One evening the officers of the Battalion were all together outside the mess tent having supper and chatting. There were still black out conditions although the war had now moved to Sicily and Southern Italy. My Anti-Tank Platoon was camped uncomfortably close to the Battalion HQ mess tent and I was a little concerned that they would do something awful and be detected by the CO and the other officers present. Sure enough, a sheet of flame appeared from the Anti-Tank area which lit up the countryside for miles around – evidently whilst brewing up they had upset a can of petrol or paraffin which had caught fire. The CO shouted to me: 'For God's sake put that fire out'.

I nonchalantly turned round in my chair with a drink in my hand and yelled; 'Have a care, fellows'. The fire was promptly extinguished. For some weeks afterwards the Platoon Commander was dubbed 'Have a care Hugo'.

Then one day the Battalion was ordered to get ready to move off immediately. We embarked on a ship and headed for Italy. By this time Sicily had been overrun by the Allies and a successful, but bloody, battle had taken place at Salerno. The Battalion disembarked at Taranto and from there it was transported to a camp near Bari on the east coast. This move coincided with Christmas and, although some special fare was known to be coming along for the festive dinner, the Colonel and I decided that we would add a fish course to the officers' mess meal. We therefore set off to the nearest river, an attractive little watercourse that looked like an English trout stream.

We arrived armed with a good supply of hand grenades and the fishing expedition was most successful. A deep pool was selected and when the grenade exploded underwater the fish were stunned and came to the surface. Being the junior officer, I had to strip off and quickly collect what fish I could before they recovered. It was very cold work. The winter weather in

Italy can be most hostile. A goodly basketful was collected, enough for each officer to have a decent sized fish for his second course. While we were certainly not eating trout (having a great number of bones and little taste) the addition of a second course, together with an issue of wine and whisky, added to the occasion and an enjoyable time was had by all.

The Division's next role was shrouded in mystery and secrecy until certain officers were ordered to Caserta, north of Naples, for a briefing. The secret was out. We were to be part of a strong force composed of British and American troops under the command of an American general to land at Anzio. Initially there was little opposition and the bridge head expanded. But it was not long before the Germans reacted with shells and gunfire from the hills overlooking the bridge head. I was in a leading column travelling along the only road towards the railway line and the hills in the distance. At one moment I was talking to a fellow officer in a Carrier and the next I was blown off my feet and sitting quite unhurt at the edge of the road – a near miss by a shell. It was surprising that no-one was injured.

Each company was engaged in various actions and generally we achieved our objectives although there was considerable confusion at nightfall and fairly heavy casualties. That night, unaware of the position, I went forward with my batman to see what lay ahead with the idea of placing some of my anti-tank guns up front. We came across a railway line with a number of scattered goods trucks. To our amazement there was a hubbub of conversation on the other side of the trucks. They were Germans, only a few yards away. Feeling that discretion was the better part of valour, I withdrew stealthily along the route I had come up. It was later discovered that I had penetrated, by accident, further forward than any other soldier in the task force until the final breakout some months later.

By dawn I had met up with my colleagues and got my guns into position some distance back from the railway line, all the time being under quite heavy shell fire. That evening, on a tour of the gun sites with my sergeant, I found one very exposed gun was unmanned. We hunted around for the crew and found them some distance away lurking in a cave. Evidently the gun had been pinpointed by the German artillery and mortars and had received heavy stonking. At the time, in my view, this was a very serious offence – abandoning a six-pounder – so I drew my revolver, placed the barrel in the back of the gun-crew leader, and escorted them to their rightful position. On arrival at the gun site some more heavy and accurate shelling descended upon us and my sergeant and one other man were hit. They were escorted back to the field dressing station and the gun was manhandled back to a safer position out of sight of the enemy. Later that night I walked back to the forward dressing station to visit my sergeant, who was badly wounded, to find out if there was anything he wanted before he was taken away.

'Yes,' he said, 'I dropped my pipe when I got hit, could you get it?'

Sergeant Bufton, a regular solider hailing from Hereford, was a wonderfully cool, reliable character whose hallmark was his hooked pipe, done up with sticking plaster. I had no alternative and I trudged back to that hostile place and by sheer good luck found the pipe and returned it to the sergeant who was immensely grateful. He was evacuated to Naples, and eventually invalided out of the Army. Regretfully, we never met up again.

By this time the Germans had assembled a strong force including tanks on the hills overlooking the beach head. During the night elements had infiltrated between the forward troops and in the general confusion it seemed quite likely that we could be encircled and cut off. My batman, Paddy, had selected a pigsty as his Platoon Headquarters and, in spite of the smell, made it as comfortable as possible. Early next morning, just after dawn, the resourceful Paddy produced a mug of hot sweet tea and a fried egg on a tin plate which he had scrounged from somewhere. One of our six-pounder guns was positioned and dug in, to some extent, fifteen yards from the pigsty with the barrel poking out from the remains of an old barn towards the open countryside.

When the two of us were about to eat our breakfast we heard the unmistakable sound of approaching tanks. I went to investigate and observed at least six tanks lumbering along at right angles to my position. Their gun turrets were swivelling around in all directions, but they had not fired as yet. I had not seen this type of tank before and concluded they must be Germans. I immediately put through a message by field telephone to Battalion HQ, only a short distance away, to tell them that German tanks were approaching and that I was about to open fire.

The reply came back 'Don't fire – tanks not yet identified'. By now I was quite convinced they were enemy tanks so I decided to take matters into my own hands. But returning to the gun by the pigsty I found that the gun crew had disappeared, presumably taking cover somewhere. So I manned the gun myself, since there was no time to be lost, with the faithful Irishman behind me thrusting shells into the breech block. The first few shots really scared my own troops who were dug in some depth in front of the gun. The armour-plated shells whizzed over their heads by no more than a foot or two. They were not sure where the shots were coming from – us or them?

I was well trained in gunnery, but the first few shots were wide of the mark. It was quite difficult to tell the range. Soon I got on target with one near miss over and one near miss under. I had achieved the bracket. Now I started to demolish the tanks and soon had done in four. Some of them were knocked out and I could see the tank crews leaping out and running to safety. By this time another bigger gun, an Anti-Tank Regiment seventeen-pounder, situated some distance away, opened up and scored quite a number of hits. The attack was repulsed and the remaining tanks could be seen disappearing at top speed in the direction from which they had come.

I had quite enjoyed this encounter; the gun had been well placed so that I was able to hit the tanks sideways on. Although the Germans fired a few shots back, fortunately for me nothing was returned directly at my gun. After this engagement my first thought was that I had at least personally avenged my brother's death when flying with the RAF over Albania.

Later on, I was to receive an American Silver Star for gallantry with the citation reading as follows:-

> HUGH RIPLEY, 156685, Captain, The King's Own Shropshire Light Infantry, British Army, for gallantry in action on the Anzio Beach head from 29 January to 4 February 1944. During the Allied Attack on 29 January the Captain commanded the anti-tank guns of his battalion, and by thorough and

> aggressive reconnaissance he kept his guns in extremely close support of the foremost assault elements. Moving them forward under heavy enemy fire, his inspiring leadership and complete disregard of his own life and safety spurred his command to move by hand those important artillery pieces across shell-swept approaches to new positions. Later on 4 February when the enemy attempted to penetrate the Allied lines, the Captain personally manned one of his own guns and destroyed four German Mark IV tanks. That night the enemy attack increased and the entire battalion was ordered to withdraw and break off contact. Although the Germans had already seized some positions near the line of withdrawal, Captain Ripley again demonstrated extreme courage and outstanding devotion to duty in supervising the extrication of seven guns which were in danger of capture. Despite painful wounds which he incurred during the end of this action he did not leave the area until the last gun had been safely extricated. Entered service from Bedstone, Bucknell, Shropshire, England.

As it turned out it was just as well that I disobeyed orders when told not to fire for undoubtedly the Division, or at least the forward elements of it, would have been encircled and overrun. Indeed there were already German troops in the rear of my position, unknown at the time, for the tanks to link up with. This came to light later in the day when a long line of British prisoners were seen quite close by being marched off under German escort towards their own lines. This was too much for Peter, a gallant Company Commander, who leapt into a carrier and recaptured them. In spite of these set-backs, the Germans seemed intent on wiping out the beach head salient. The shelling became intense, and there was no doubt that something else was afoot. British and American forces were indeed very vulnerable.

Orders were given to withdraw that evening back to a line nearer to the sea. I succeeded in extracting my guns ready for redeployment further back. But when conducting operations with my men and vehicles on the road out there was another very heavy and accurate burst of shelling. I dived into a ditch; to my cost, others were doing the same. There was another fellow under me in the ditch so I was still half exposed. The next thing I remember was an appalling noise and a shattering blow to my head and face. I evidently passed out for a short time. When I came round I found blood oozing out of the left side of my face. I couldn't see out of one eye and my mouth seemed to be full of stuff. I spat and a mass of blood, teeth and metal came out. A piece of the shell had gone through my cheek, broken the sinus bone, and ripped out a lot of teeth.

Someone was kind enough to wrap a field dressing round my face and convey me to a carrier which went through the smoke and debris at speed and dropped me at the field dressing station a mile or two back. The tented area was jam-packed with casualties and, of course, within easy reach of the enemy artillery; but although shells fell round about they seemed to respect the prominent Red Cross signs. I was transferred from a stretcher to a bed and soon received attention from a nurse who was most cheerful and a good morale booster. A cup of tea was passed around but I couldn't cope with that so a tea pot was produced and a welcome brew was poured down my throat from the spout.

The Padre was the next visitor. He had been travelling round the beds with a cheerful word to everyone. When he reached me, he said: 'Cheer up – have a cigarette'. A cigarette was duly lit and I had a puff. I detected that the Padre was looking at me in rather a curious way; eventually he remarked: 'You know you will remember this. I expect it will be the first and last time that smoke comes out of your cheek when you smoke a cigarette'. I guffawed painfully, but it restored me once again to normality.

The next day I was taken off on a stretcher and ended up aboard a hospital ship in Anzio harbour. I was on the deck for quite a while and wondered if my luck was going to hold. Shells from 'Big Bertha', a German railway gun, were dropping all around. I was most relieved when the ship got under way. The short voyage to Naples was uneventful and I was transported to a general hospital on a hill overlooking the Bay of Naples and Mount Vesuvius. It was subsequently learnt that although the Battalion was engaged in heavy fighting it withdrew according to plan and the Germans failed in their attempt to obliterate the bridge head.

I was operated on quite soon after my arrival and made a good recovery. Teeth were in some disarray and the sinus gave trouble but I could see all right and my face had been stitched up. I was once again mobile and felt how lucky I was compared to some of the badly wounded in the ward. The man in the next door bed to me had lost both his eyes. Although given sedatives he screamed and yelled and frantically tore at the bandages around his head. He died, which was a merciful release. Another man close by was a Lieutenant in my outfit, a member of the Marks and Spencer family. All the original Company Commanders had been killed or wounded and he had been an acting Company Commander. I went over to talk to him and gave him a lighted cigarette. He smoked and talked faintly, then died quite peacefully. He had multiple injuries and there was little chance that he would survive.

Looking out of the hospital window a magnificent sight presented itself, particularly at night. Vesuvius had decided to erupt. This was in February, 1944, and it was the last time the crater really became active. The boiling lava slowly and relentlessly rolled down the mountain, wave upon wave, and destroyed everything in its path. Houses on the foothills went down like a pack of cards and many aeroplanes and workshops at a war-time airstrip were engulfed. It was easy to understand the plight of Pompeii many centuries before.

I was released from hospital and given two or three weeks' convalescent leave at Sorrento. I was by now perfectly fit and well, other than an unsightly, healed up, cavity in my face. Being quite vain I covered this up with a bit of plaster and had a very enjoyable holiday in Southern Italy with frequent trips to Capri. Fortunately there was an abundance of female company available. Next door to the fine hotel in which I was billeted under the auspices of the White Cross the Americans had taken over another hotel as a rest area for American nurses.

The holiday ended when a truck arrived to return me to the Naples hospital for a face correction. This was duly performed by an eminent British plastic surgeon. It was said that the cavity was filled up with Neapolitan after-birth. The wound healed up and I looked more or less normal again. I was left with a small dent in my face which I have to this day. It looked like a sabre wound from a duel.

Again I was mobile and ready for action. I went to the La Scala Opera House, which was still giving performances; indeed they had never stopped – Naples having been over-run and therefore undamaged by the war. There were some fine officers' clubs in Naples at that time with entertainment and dances with no shortage of off-duty nurses, both American and British. Down by the port, where there are now many good seafood restaurants, other forms of entertainment were available. Pimps, thieving boys and tarts abounded. Talk about 'See Naples and die' – the saying could well have derived from the activities in that area. All the girls, some very attractive, suffered from VD, so careful precautions had to be taken. They were all very poor yet cheerful amongst the squalor.

Having fully recovered I was told to report to a transit camp on the outskirts of Naples. I duly registered and collected mess tin, tin cup and knife, fork and spoon, and made up any other deficiencies in kit. I was shown an inhospitable bell tent with long grass growing within, and was told that was my home until further notice. There was a motley collection of soldiery wandering around aimlessly. Some of them had been there a long time and found it a convenient way of escaping any theatre of war. It was not my cup of tea at all, so I decided to escape, go missing, and make my way down to the port. I was missing my mates in the Battalion. After chatting up one or two ships' captains I succeeded in hitching a lift back to Anzio.

My friends were surprised at my return, yet very pleased to see me. The Adjutant remarked that he would have to do a bit of fiddling with the records as I was no longer on the Battalion strength. Soon I was up in the line again in very scary and uncomfortable places like the 'Boot' and the 'Starfish'. This was static warfare, each side being in very close proximity. Mortar bombs rained down from both sides and snipers were very active, should a head appear over the top. Indeed at a forward listening post Germans could be heard talking about fifty yards way. They were dug in with wire and mines round about them and could not be got at unless there was a major push.

It was the turn of my Company to be relieved and return to the rest area. This was always done at night and as quietly as possible; in spite of these precautions there were always quite a few casualties from mortar bombs. The rest area was in the woods not far from Anzio town (if you can call it that; there was nothing there but ruins) and they were still vulnerable from Big Bertha and enemy aircraft. The area consisted of a series of underground shelters. Every man made his own dugout with a roof on the top to avoid being blown up by delayed anti-personnel bombs (the size of a billiard ball) which were dropped at night by enemy aircraft.

One morning I woke up with the sun streaming into my dugout. I thought to myself that this was strange. Paddy, the batman, should have been in by this time with a cup of tea. I got up and went off to Paddy's shelter, only a few yards away, thinking that he had probably overslept. To my horror I found Paddy dead in his make-shift bunk. An anti-personnel bomb had rolled down the entrance of his dugout and exploded inside.

It was time to go up the line again. I now found myself as Signals Officer – not that I knew much about it. One encounter I remember clearly was when I was on my way up to the forward positions travelling along a crawl trench – the whole place was festooned with them to prevent unnecessary casualties from shell bursts. Along a stretch of the trench I found myself face to face with a venomous looking green snake. The Anzio area was known to be inhabited by a variety of poisonous snakes. I was never sure whether I or the snake was more scared. At that time there was fairly heavy shelling and I was reluctant to expose myself – yet the snake took up an aggressive attitude and would not clear out of the way. In the end I decided to give the snake best, and I leapt out into the open during a lull in the shelling, sprinted along, by-passing the snake and returned to the comparative safety of the crawl trench.

The breakout was imminent, scheduled to coincide with a final attack on Monte Cassino. Ironically, the Anzio landing had been supposed to cut off the German forces in the Cassino area months before. Before the final advance I discovered an American Jeep which had been upended in a minefield and had been abandoned. I felt that this might be a suitable means of transport to Rome if I could get it out so, with the help of the transport officer, who provided tracked vehicles and hawser, the Jeep was successfully extracted; furthermore it was in fine working order. I retained it for many months and it proved to be a most useful vehicle especially in Rome when that particular battle was over.

The battalion spent the next month or two in relative luxury about twenty miles from Rome. It was a tented camp in a pretty valley in which olive and cypress trees were dotted about. Discipline was relaxed to some extent and it was the intention that all ranks should rest and recuperate after months of continuous engagement under constant shellfire. There is no doubt that a number of men had become 'bomb-happy' and it would take some little time for them to recover. There was transport laid on for all ranks to go to and from Rome at will – provided they were smart and properly dressed. I was now well placed with my private Jeep and spent most of my time in the city getting to know many charming Roman families. The five star Excelsior Hotel had been taken over by the Americans and it was in full working order with bars, Turkish baths and restaurants – though offering a limited menu because food was scarce in Rome at that time. The Army with their rations were much better off in that respect than the local inhabitants.

One evening I found myself at a party in the Excelsior where a number of the guests were Italian – some of whom had probably been entertained by the Germans a week or two previously. Yet the Italians were truly happy about the belated entry of the Allies into their capital and went out of their way to be friendly and hospitable. I spied a very pretty young girl. She was animated and talked perfect English and was accompanied by a large black poodle. I thought to myself, I must meet this girl so I went over and patted the dog – a ploy I had found to be quite successful in the past. Francesca, as she was called, and I had been talking for some moments when I noticed a distinguished looking man wearing an Old Etonian tie. I indicated my astonishment and asked if she knew him. She said: 'Yes, that's my father, come and meet him'.

He was in fact a Roman Prince of ancient lineage who had indeed been educated at Eton. This chance meeting led to a close friendship with the family who lived in a large and beautiful villa off Via Garibaldi, overlooking the Vatican. Francesca and I met up every day during this rest period and in the months ahead, once the advance had got going again, I invariably stayed at the villa when I was out of the line and had a week or so's leave. At this time I drove around everywhere in my captured Jeep accompanied by Francesca, for whom I had written out and signed a formal looking pass giving her permission to be driven in WD vehicles. We were quite often stopped by the military police who asked to see her pass but they never queried the authenticity of this spurious document.

Some days we would motor off to the outskirts of Rome and have a game of golf, stopping *en route* to meet some of her relations. On other occasions I would collect her from the villa and go off for a day's trout-fishing around Tivoli, having borrowed the Prince's trout rod and equipment. It was a good life while it lasted. Officers of the Battalion hired a spacious flat in the centre of Rome where they entertained their friends and where they kept a good supply of food and drink. Francesca and I spent many agreeable hours there.

At this time I was sent off on a short signals course since I was now the fully fledged Signals Officer. I put the knowledge gained there to full use by fixing up a direct line from my tent to Francesca's bedroom at the villa.

Now the rest period was over and it was time to chase after the Germans again. Bonzo, a pure-bred fox terrier, had been added to the establishment. He was a present from Francesca on leaving Rome. The little dog soon settled down to Army life and became a great favourite with the fellows. Action returned suddenly and dramatically. Florence had been declared an open city yet most of the bridges other than the Ponte Vecchio had been destroyed. German guns positioned just north of the city started to open up accurately on the road which runs alongside the south of the Arno. Unfortunately I had to take over a signals headquarters from the Gurkhas which in itself was bad enough since there was a complete language barrier; but worse, in the course of my duties, I had to travel regularly along the road – in all about a mile – which had been pinpointed by the German gunners.

I decided that the best mode of conveyance would be an Army motorbike. Some very scary trips were made at high speed dodging the shells. It was a bit like a game of Ludo – once over the Ponte Vecchio I was home and safe. I was blown off my bike once and had to avoid new craters on each trip. There was also a nasty feeling of being alone. There was no other traffic. In spite of running the gauntlet many times I got through unscathed.

There was no lingering in Florence. The Germans were on the run and speed was essential. I had been given command of a Company and promoted Major. The country to the north of Florence was rugged, hilly and sparsely populated. The only sign of life was an occasional farm house. The company bashed on, covering many miles on foot, with a few nasty encounters *en route* and some casualties. We had over-run the supply lines, indeed there were no roads, so there was no chance of the daily rations coming up. We lived off the land as best we could. At one barn recently evacuated by the Germans, crates of dry biscuits had been left behind. These were distributed and kept the troops going for the next few days.

Whenever possible I made my temporary headquarters at a farm house. The Italian farmers were more than hospitable and insisted on sharing their meals. Also these havens were warm and the bad weather was just starting. These smallholdings, situated on the side of a mountain, were constructed in such a way that the cattle occupied the bottom floor and the heat generated by the beasts warmed up the whole house.

C-Company were set for another attack. The Battalion Commander came up, issued orders from a map as it was getting dark, and told the various Company Commanders to get going. I set off with my merry men, tired but in good spirits. I was ordered to capture a mountain miles away and hold it. This was one of the few times that a Company Commander really had to lead his men. There was no question of putting scouts out in front because it was dark and they wouldn't know where to go. It was a question of just taking a chance and hoping the enemy were not there. We reached our objective and dug in. When dawn arrived I took stock of the situation and found that I had captured the wrong mountain!

In the end we arrived at the right place and again dug in. I decided to make my headquarters in the bank of a dry river bed and as night approached went to sleep. I was woken up by the noise of roaring torrents all around me. Indeed there was torrential rain and evidently there had been severe storms in the mountains. We were wet through and had to evacuate. As luck would have it there was a small village with a large farmstead nearby. The troops were able to dry out and were given chickens and turkeys by the locals. But this was only a small respite. My headquarters, in a large barn-like area which constituted the main farm house, were macabre and smelly. An old lady had died there a few weeks before and was lying on a bed in a corner. The locals had not been able to move her away. There was a great deal of weeping and wailing and chanting.

We were soon on the move again and were shortly to become engaged in a nasty little battle. The rear guard of the main German Army were skilled in delaying operations – they held on to a dominant position to the last possible moment, causing maximum havoc before withdrawing – and my Company were to be caught in one of these traps. I had positioned one of my platoons on a bare hillside with orders for them to dig in. The ground was hard and rocky and whilst the men were frantically busy with their entrenching tools the Germans must have observed this activity and plastered the hill with mortar and shell fire. I managed to move most of them out to a safer place, but some were killed whilst in the process of digging and still clutching their entrenching tools.

I also had a near escape in this encounter. I was crawling forward through some long bushy grass to see what lay ahead when a machine gun opened up at quite short range. I hugged the earth and the bullets went ripping through the grass above my head. I managed to get a message through to my own mortars which opened rapid fire and dislodged the enemy.

Kesselring's German forces now withdrew north and established themselves in some strength around the Futa Pass area with their backs to Bologna and the Po Valley. I was to spend Christmas, 1944, up there. The Appenines in winter are not to be recommended. But first we were to be pulled out of the line after our rapid advance and were put into a rest area a little north of Florence. This was a very happy two or three weeks' respite. Florence was comparatively undamaged and life went on there as usual. I made a number of visits to this beautiful city and also managed to obtain a week's leave of absence to stay with Francesca at Villa Ruspoli in Rome.

One evening I went off in a truck to Florence with some fellow soldiers. I and a friend became involved in a party and after consuming far too much alcohol decided to turn our attention to the Florentine girls that were present. One lady complained about a severe pain so I mischievously suggested I should take her home and, as a doctor, give her an examination. This I duly did. The girl disrobed and I prodded around in what I considered to be an expert way. After a little time she was most appreciative and said she was cured. This seemed to be a sign of approval so I too disrobed and spent the night with her.

Now the problems arose. I had missed the truck to take me back to camp and there was a Battalion parade at eight thirty am. I had no transport and was in a fix. By good fortune I waved down a vegetable lorry on the route north. There was no room in the front so I lay down in the back amongst the cabbages, melons, sprouts and tomatoes. To my horror as we came alongside the camp I saw the full Battalion on parade with the CO Bill Hulton-Harrop marching on to take the salute. There was a noticeable gap in front of C-Company where I should have been standing to attention in front of my men. I leapt off the lorry in full view of everyone, my clothes in some disarray and covered with vegetable matter. I brushed myself down, collected myself, and marched smartly to my allotted place in front of my company. The inspection was duly carried out and I managed to get away with it – although there was a lot of good natured ribbing in the mess afterwards.

The final chapter of my soldiering in Italy took on a new turn. I was beginning to think that my mountaineering training on the Atlas mountains in Algeria had not perhaps been wasted after all. Before taking over our positions on the Appenines, away up in the high mountains, we were issued with string vests and white cotton cloaks – for camouflage against the snow background – and mules for transport. My troops were spread out along a large range of high mountains and I myself settled into the ruin of an old farm house, which came to be known as Stonk House. There was intermittent shelling from big guns and the house had been hit a few times.

The cellar of the house was fairly safe so our Headquarters staff all crammed in there. We were in there one evening when there was an almighty explosion. After the dust and smoke started to clear I looked around to explore the extent of the damage. It transpired that a dozy signalman had been playing around with a live grenade and by mistake pulled out the pin. Fortunately he had the presence of mind to fling it to an unoccupied part of the room and miraculously no-one was hit by the splinters.

I and my new batman, Tom, went upstairs to observe what was going on. To our surprise a large white pig galloped past the window through the mist, evidently terrified by the shells that were exploding regularly round about. Tom in peacetime had worked in a slaughterhouse in Cornwall. Without a moment's hesitation he leapt through the open window – the glass had gone a long time ago – and gave chase, brandishing an evil-looking flick knife. About half an hour later Tom was observed through the mist dragging along the dead pig. He had cornered it and cut its throat. Tom spent the day butchering it and presents of meat were given to the companies alongside. Some extra shelling had to be endured that evening while bits of the pig were being cooked. The Germans had noticed smoke coming out of the chimney. Yet there was great celebration that night when the troops dined on roast pork.

There was always considerable confusion and activity in the rear areas where wheeled supplies were transferred to the mules at night time. These operations were under the control of the Regimental Sergeant-Major. He was a huge fellow, fairly thick, but did the job well. Davies, his driver, told the story of one occasion when the RSM, whose headquarters was further back, was called forward unexpectedly to the mule loading point. Davies was maintaining the Jeep and had the plugs out. He told the RSM he couldn't go for this reason whereupon the RSM, in a fit of rage, yelled out: 'Bugger the plugs, throw them in the back and get going!'

It was a bad evening for the RSM. When they did eventually get to the loading point in the dark, one joker, probably on purpose, tried to throw a saddle onto his back. He was not best pleased and shouted 'Get off it – what do you think I am – a bloody mule'.

Early one morning when the mule train was on its way back from Stonk House I and George, one of my Platoon Commanders, had to transport a body back to the rear area for burial. We had planned to throw the poor chap over the mule and tie him on. Unfortunately *rigor mortis* had set in and with the Arctic weather he was as stiff as a board. We made many attempts to strap him on but he kept falling off and the mule was taking great exception to the whole proceedings. In the end we tied the fellow on securely lengthways with his head by the mule's shoulders and the legs protruding out above the tail. Although the Cypriot muleteer was last seen struggling with the crazed mule, who was bucking and leaping about, the body was apparently safely delivered for burial. As it happened this dead chap was a comic with a great sense of humour, so George and I liked to think that his final journey, under somewhat unusual and at times hilarious conditions, was not altogether inappropriate.

My company was moved further along the mountainside and closer to the church which dominated a prominent position. It was a static situation and, being a much wider front, was not nearly so scary as the weeks spent in the waddis at Anzio. Most nights I would go out with a small patrol dressed in their white cloaks to reconnoitre. It was bitterly cold, often snowing, and always with a thick layer of snow on the ground. It was an eerie experience yet very beautiful on a still night with a full moon. We never ran into an enemy post, indeed we never really knew where they were – presumably dug in on the other side of the mountains since my company was within range of its infantry mortar bombs. On returning to my dugout I had to spend some time de-freezing. Snow drifted on my moustache and had frozen solid.

On Christmas Day, 1944, special rations came up. In addition to a rum ration for the troops I was sent a bottle of white wine by my CO. But my dugout was not exactly the Ritz: there were inches of water at the bottom of the trench and most of the troops were suffering from some form of trench foot or minor frost bite – but we made the best of it. At least there was no firing from either side for the day. An unofficial truce had been declared. Indeed at about midday the Germans rang the church bells to indicate that they had no hostile intentions on that day.

Before being relieved by the Americans I had a lucky escape. I had moved my headquarters further up the mountain into a niche in the rocks so as to supervise the take over. I had given orders that at 'X' hour all the ammunition should be fired. I felt that I would like to give the enemy a proper farewell and there didn't seem to be much point in taking the stuff back again. The Americans duly arrived, masses of them, making a dreadful noise at about daybreak. Instead of manhandling ammunition and supplies up the rocky tracks, they brought the laden mules right up to the forward positions. All hell broke out. The Germans opened up with everything they had got. I felt a thump over my heart, which turned out to be a piece of shrapnel which had gone through my battle dress pocket and ended up inside my metal cigarette case: a lucky break.

My Company Sergeant-Major was hit and there were one or two other casualties. I decided to get out with all possible speed and leave the Yanks to it. Thus ended my active service in Italy.

10

Picking Up the Pieces

Fairly regular correspondence had been carried on with the girl from Scotland whom I had met at Callander before embarkation to Africa and also with Diana, though the letters were not so frequent from her. There were also strong rumours in Rome that I had become engaged to the Princess. This was quite unfounded and I had no intention of getting married while the war was on. In fact I never saw Francesca again for twenty-five years until she was over in London and staying at the Ritz.

Two of my brothers had now been killed in the war. Derek had been shot down over Albania when flying a Gloucester Gladiator in the RAF and Edward, a Battalion Commander, was killed at Caen soon after the Allied landing in Normandy. He was married and a daughter was born posthumously. A sister, Ruth, who was an auxiliary nurse throughout the war, also died in her early thirties. So I, from a family of six children, was left with just a younger brother, Nigel, and sister, Suzan.

Back on the line, my Battalion moved leisurely south, stopping at such interesting places as Perugia and Citta del Piavi until we embarked from Taranto to Beirut. The purpose of this exercise was to be available and if necessary to be called in to fight should the trouble between the French and Syrians/ Lebanese become out of hand. I and the Battalion motored in convoy over the mountains until we arrived at Damascus Racecourse, where camp was set up. All companies had areas to look after to ensure that law and order was being kept. Troops had not been to this part before so the locals were curious and the Arab Sheikhs, feeling it would be best to get on with these intruders, tended to bestow gifts and hospitality.

On the very first day, a fine looking Arab found his way to my headquarters with a magnificent white Arab stallion. The Arab explained that the stallion was for my personal use for the time I was stationed in his locality. Every morning the horse was produced and taken away in the evening. It was a remarkable animal: while perfectly trained in dressage, it was ridden with only a halter to which reins were attached. Evidently it had never been introduced to a bit. I had a great time riding round my company positions every day and sometimes going for longer trips out into the desert to look for gazelle.

Some days, with a friend and two Arab hunters, I would go off deep into the desert in a Jeep to course gazelle. Once we had sighted one we would go at full throttle to try to catch up with the animal which could travel at up to forty miles an hour. We succeeded in shooting one or two with a service rifle, but more often than not the gazelle got away. It was an exciting yet a fairly dangerous sport. The terrain was rough and uncertain and sometimes when going flat out a deep waddi would appear only yards ahead. With a screech of brakes and clouds of dust the steering wheel was yanked round – the technique being to skid the Jeep and thus avoid disaster.

In front of my headquarters, yet some distance away near the foothills of the mountains, there was a wired-in ammunition dump which I was supposed to keep an eye on. At dawn one morning I noticed a suspicious-looking group of Arabs with a donkey close to this compound. I immediately alerted a section of men and went after them. The thieving Arabs were too smart for me and got away, but they had to leave the donkey behind. A good donkey is quite a valuable and prized possession in those parts and I added it to the company strength. It accompanied me on many subsequent moves through Palestine and into Egypt where it was eventually sold for quite a good sum of money which went to company funds.

Damascus City was a quaint and smelly old place and there was not much entertainment for the troops. They did, however, clinch some good bargains in buying lengths of silk which they stuffed into their kit bags as presents for wives and girlfriends when they eventually got back home. I also did well in this respect. It was a strange sight to see the old men sitting around the narrow streets of the town smoking their hubbly-bubblies. I sat with them sometimes to have a smoke. It didn't seem to do me any harm or give me a kick – yet there is no doubt they were smoking opium.

I was asked out to a feast by the local sheikhs. The location was a settlement some miles away through the desert. Everyone squatted around a huge fire laden with food which included mountains of rice, sheep, chickens, venison and other tasty bits and pieces. The idea was to dig in with your fingers and gorge. Being the principal guest I opened the feast by being offered and accepting a sheep's eye – considered to be a great delicacy. It looked nasty but I put a brave face on it and swallowed, swiftly chasing the morsel down with mouthfuls of tasty food to obliterate this unusual gastronomic experience. At the end of the meal the Arabs were belching well and the feast finished with countless tiny cups of aromatic black coffee.

Beirut, forty miles away, was a very much more civilized city. The French were still there and although they were beginning to depart they had left their mark in the shape of excellent restaurants, high class brothels and, in the Arab Quarter, belly dancers and more sophisticated entertainment. The drawback was that it was very expensive – usually the case wherever there is a French influence. One evening myself and Lester Otter-Barry, the acting Colonel, were invited to a party on a cruiser lying alongside at Beirut. The Navy entertained us in their usual hospitable manner with a cabaret, a magnificent buffet supper, and drinks of all description. The two of us proceeded to get nicely smashed.

At a late hour the party finished and Leicester, well in his cups and becoming rather aggressive, told the driver of his staff car to get out of his seat and he would drive the vehicle home. I, on the other hand, was equally certain that I was not going to be driven back over the mountains to Damascus by Lester – a dangerous trip at the best of times. A fierce argument ensued and as there seemed to be no other solution to the problem; I clocked him a good one and he was removed into the back seat. The usual nine am Battalion parade took place on the racecourse next day. Lester, taking the salute, appeared looking shaky and with a magnificent black eye – a real shiner. It is quite a serious offence to hit your Commanding Officer; but Lester, a real gent and a very gallant man, took no action. It was only some weeks later, when recalling our various exploits in the mess, that Lester said: 'Hugo, you did me a good turn when you clouted me after the Naval party at Beirut'.

All the vehicles were loaded up including the donkey, which was heaved into the back of a three-tonner by the troops, and the Battalion moved on to Palestine. The Jews did their best to pre-empt the Balfour Declaration Act – that Palestine was to become a national home for Jews – and eventually succeeded. At this time there were sparodic incidents, such as blowing up WD vehicles by terrorist gangs – the Stern gang (with a certain Menachem Begin among them) being the main culprits.

The Colonel and I often went out duck shooting in marshy country around Acre. Passing through the various settlements, more often than not we would see squads of youths both male and female, being drilled by a professional and being trained for forthcoming battles. Arms were short in these days so they were issued with mock-up rifles made with wood. Yet it was a sure sign of the Jews' warlike intentions.

Of more concern to myself and my troops were the activities of the Palestinian Arabs. In spite of lookouts and wire all around the perimeter of the camp, the Arabs found their way into the tents at night and stole anything they could lay their hands on. When punished, they had been known to take revenge. The primitive latrine sites within the compound were an area of danger and extra vigilance was necessary. Incidents had occurred when a soldier taken short at night and squatting down to attend to the needs of nature had his testicles removed with a sharp knife.

The real troubles, however, had not started at this stage. Palestine was still one of the most agreeable places to be stationed; Tel Aviv was a busy and exciting city mostly inhabited by Jews. Jerusalem, Haifa, and areas round the Sea of Galilee were beautiful and of great historic interest – and they were all within easy striking distance of Nathania Camp where I was stationed. Lake Hula, north of the Sea of Galilee, was one of the best duck shoots in the world. Early morning and evening flighting would account for big bags. The Guns would get into their hides in the rushes around the huge lake with one or two Arab boys. At the end of the flight these lads would leap into the water and retrieve the game – and there was little they missed.

Another pastime was to go out hunting with the Ramile

Vale. The hounds hunted jackal, and I was mounted on an old charger. In that area there were fields for the cattle and sheep surrounded by cactus hedges which made admirable jumps: the horses had learnt to lift their feet up and take no liberties. The sturdy thorns were an inch or two long and became poisonous when embedded in the flesh.

On the work front my company was sent off on detachment to guard the oil pipe line against saboteurs. This was quite a cushy job and entailed a series of inter-communicating posts with night patrols to deter any intruders. The only trouble encountered was the usual loss of kit to the thieving Arabs who crawled under the tent flaps at night.

Things tended to happen suddenly and for no accountable reason. Overnight instructions were given for the Battalion to entrain, its destination being the Bitter Lakes, with a stop *en route* at Gaza for a hot meal. Moascar Barracks was a proper peacetime barracks with permanent buildings and all the amenities that go with it, including some good sailing. More important, so far as I and my friends were concerned, it was within striking distance of Cairo and Alexandria. Short leave was easy to get and, in any event, parades and training programmes were finished at the latest by midday because of the heat.

The legendary Shepheards Hotel in Cairo was the usual rendezvous. It was a very gracious establishment with the staff dressed up in their colourful Egyptian robes – they were tall people, who moved very slowly but with great dignity. Shepheards Bar was known internationally and lived up to its name. There many missions dotted around Cairo, particularly on Gezira, an up-market island in the middle of the Nile, populated by rich Egyptians, diplomats, and senior service officers attached to Embassies and the like, who had enjoyed a good war, and were understandably reluctant to leave. After a game of polo, a swim, a game of squash or tennis at the club they would often repair to the bar with their secretaries or girl friends.

At about this time I received papers notifying me that I was eligible for 'Class B' release from the Army. I was still on the books with my old company in Ceylon; indeed my employers had been very generous in paying me a small amount throughout my absence on war service. Planting tea was classified as of national importance so I had the opportunity of accelerated release now the war was over. In the event I decided to give up my career in Ceylon. My mother and father had suffered severe shocks in losing two sons and a daughter during the war years. I felt that I should remain near at hand to help them in any way I could and assist in running the estate in Shropshire.

It was a happy day when I collected my demob suit at the depot and I experienced little trouble in adjusting to civilian life and resuming country pursuits. Yet I felt strangely unfulfilled. I had never been one for hanging around long and doing nothing; I felt that I must embark on a new career and get married. Regrettably my first girl friend Diana had hitched up with a squadron leader in my absence. This did not prevent me seeing a lot of her, during these postwar months but the situation was unsatisfactory. I turned my attentions elsewhere in the search for a suitable female.

Among the likely runners Ursula seemed entertaining – half-spanish and tending to be rather fiery. On one occasion I took her out to dinner at the old Berkeley Hotel in Piccadilly. Immediately after the war hotels did a thriving business and it was difficult to secure a table. During dinner a fish bone stuck in Ursula's throat. All the usual remedies were called upon, such as hitting her on the back, swallowing bread, drinking water, but to no avail. She lost her colour and started choking. There was no doubt that it was a hospital job. Equally I was reluctant to vacate the table; if I left there would be no chance of getting into the restaurant again during that busy time. Besides the menu looked good. I gave directions to Ursula as to how to get to St George's Hospital on Hyde Park Corner and despatched her to have the fish-bone removed with instructions that she was to return when she was all right again.

Meanwhile I remained at the table, being fortified at frequent intervals by a succession of beverages. Ursula returned in due time, none the worse for wear, and we enjoyed an excellent dinner. Although we remained good friends, somehow she never forgot my ungallant attitude towards this incident.

I always had a very soft spot for Scotland. As a boy I had been up there many times, shooting, fishing and stalking, and had also spent a couple of years in Glasgow before going out to

Ceylon. So I travelled north to see the girl I had met at Callender during the early years of the war, Dorothy Bruce-Jones. After all, she had been writing to me regularly and seemed to be keen on the nuptials. The family lived in a large house with a staff and I was made extremely comfortable there – furthermore the father, a great old Scottish character, took a beat on a famous Scottish salmon river and invited me to fish whenever I liked. The girl was about twenty and very pretty. I at this stage was twenty-eight.

I took my time, carefully weighing up the pros and cons, and eventually decided to pop the question. I was accepted and I duly asked the father for the girl's hand. Although fairly impecunious and without a job I seemed to meet with approval.

The introduction of my fiancée to my parents' old, dilapidated country house at Bedstone was hardly the success of all time. It was a cold wet winter's day and there were buckets and basins littered around everywhere because the roof leaked – indeed as she came into the side door, the front door being jammed, she received a douche of cold water down her neck. She had never experienced anything like this before and took an instant dislike to the place. Furthermore my parents were not all that accommodating. My mother in particular scared the life out of her and my father, still attracted to pretty young girls, grabbed her whenever the opportunity occurred.

The household, what there were of them, busied themselves in the preparation of the engagement party. The now toothless Jackson – only a few weeks before his push-bike had collided on the drive with my mother's car – was put to work stoking up the boiler. The engagement party went off quite well: pretty disgusting food but plenty of drink – my father made sure of that. I was particularly pleased that Diana, whom I was to meet again under quite unusual and unexpected circumstances turned up.

The wedding took place in London. I wore my Army uniform, the bride of course wore white, attended by a strong entourage of bridesmaids and pages, mostly of Scotch descent. There was a reception at Searcy's establishment in Knightsbridge and we spent our wedding night at Grosvenor House Hotel. We went up to Scotland for the honeymoon –

foreign travel was restricted in those days – and stayed in a comfortable hotel with excellent food. Unfortunately for the bride, the hotel was situated alongside a fine salmon river and, as an ardent fisherman, I tended to push off to cast a fly at an early hour from time to time. But I returned in time for a good Scottish breakfast with porridge, followed by a kipper, and ending up with a robust mixed grill. This procedure went on for a few days until we moved on to the hotel in Callendar where we had first met.

By now I was beginning to feel that I should get some work. Jobs were offered to me by my splendid father-in-law, such as looking after farms which they had acquired, I was reluctant to become involved in any side of their family business.

Having been a most irregular soldier I knew I had the opportunity of becoming a regular soldier, provided I passed a few interviews. This was an unusual situation and applied to field officers in particular, presumably because there was a shortage of trained Army officers with war experience. So I put in an application, well supported by my CO and other influential friends, because I could not find anything else that I was competent to do. Whilst enjoying our honeymoon, now at Callendar, I received a telegram that I was to report to a headquarters at Chester at eleven am the next morning to be interviewed by the Generals. I managed to arrive there on time; but due to the disorganizations of the railways – nothing changes – I arrived scruffy and unshaven. I apologized to the smart looking Guards officers in attendance, explaining my plight and hoping that they would pass on my explanation to the Generals.

I was then ushered in. I think I saw Brownjohn to start with. Afterwards I was most certainly interviewed by Horrocks, who was a very agreeable General and was most concerned that I should have been disturbed from my honeymoon, and quite understood that I should present myself unshaven. Horrocks considered it was very bad management for the regiment to interfere with a honeymoon and mentioned that he would be in touch with the Adjutant and issue a reprimand. I got on well with the General and it was indicated there and then that they would be happy to have me as a regular soldier. Although the honeymoon had been disrupted for a bit, at least I had got a job – not particularly agreeable so far as my wife was concerned, but better than nothing.

I returned to the depot in Shropshire where I found everyone from the CO downwards was bowing and scraping. They had received a monumental rocket from the General for being inconsiderate to me during my honeymoon. Being in a fairly powerful position, and thoroughly disliking life at the depot, I opted to rejoin the Regiment in Egypt. Now that the war was finished and I had become a regular soldier I was demoted to the substantive rank of Captain. On arrival at Cairo I went straight to Shepheards Hotel where by good chance I ran into my CO, Lester Otter-Barry, the chap who I had an argument with in Beirut. There was a great re-union, with him and other friends. After a minute or two Leicester observed that I was wearing three pips on my epaulettes and wanted to know why. I remarked that I was now a regular soldier and was only a Captain.

Leicester blew up and said that may be the Army's attitude, but not his after the time we had spent together in hostile parts. He summoned an Egyptian servant and ordered him to find two crowns, which he did within a few minutes. The crowns were duly fixed on to the jacket with some ceremony. This is probably the one and only time that a soldier was actually promoted in Shepheards Bar.

On the move again, we settled in barracks in Khartoum: very hot, but not a bad posting. Sailing on the Nile, tennis, squash, shooting Egyptian geese and sand grouse, and fishing the for Nile perch (some of which were enormous and went over a hundred pounds) passed the time pleasantly enough. I was unsuccessful with rod and line, though; it wasn't the right season. But the troops , with their usual resourcefulness, managed to spear a few by standing on the dam and impaling them as they leapt upstream. At that time the British administered Khartoum so there was quite a balanced life with civilians and soldiery, although no soldiers' wives were allowed out there.

The Kahlid, Major-General Stainer, was the all important man. His jurisdiction embraced the whole of the Sudan and Eritrea. He was the Supremo, with his own aeroplane, and resided at Government House when he was not on tour. By good chance I was a great friend of his ADC, Pete, so I had an entré into the seat of power and often played tennis and dined at Government House. This proved to be very helpful because I was becoming less and less enamoured with peacetime soldiering and in perpetual training. There did not seem to be much object in anything we were doing, other than the hosepipe drill for quelling riots which was always good fun.

I had a number of altercations with my new CO 'Ikey' Reeves, a gallant soldier in the war and a regular. He was brought in from another Battalion and we had never served together before. Being accustomed to a free and easy yet adventurous life, I considered he was pernickety. The CO ran the unit on pre-war lines based on his experience in India. For example I had to march my men out to the rifle range in the desert in full pack order on a seering hot day. They were practically in a state of collapse when they arrived. Army instructions dictate that the rifle shooting test should be conducted in full clobber, wearing heavy packs, but I felt that this was impractical. Not only was the kit completely out of date – in my experience gained under war conditions – but the rules for a test on marksmanship were most likely written for a temperate climate.

I therefore told my men to divest themselves of all their heavy kit and get comfortable in the butts. There were some surprisingly good scores and instead of the exercise being an unnecessary hardship the troops enjoyed themselves, and furthermore I was able to find out who in my company were really good shots and possibly destined for a sniper's role. Unfortunately the CO decided to visit the ranges that day and was horror-struck at seeing the men shooting without their full kit. I received a severe reprimand for not obeying instructions. For future visits to the range I arranged a series of look-out posts, linked up by field telephone to alert the officer in charge of the butts of the pending arrival of the CO. This ruse worked, although it entailed a very rapid redressing operation. But we had practiced this ploy and were never caught again, so to speak, with our trousers down. In my view this was all excellent training – albeit subversive in a minor way.

I was becoming depressed and bored with the usual training routine until one morning I got up as bright as a button and in high good spirits. I walked briskly over to the Company HQ and had a cheerful word with my Company Sergeant-Major who handed me a telegram. It was from my wife, announcing that our baby had arrived – a girl, later to be christened Caroline – and that they were both well. Now I felt it was time to get back home again and to give up soldiering. This was easier said than done, having only recently rejoined as a regular, until I hit on the idea of getting the Kahlid to use his influence.

He was most sympathetic and suggested that he should put my name forward for a Company Commander's course at Warminster in Wiltshire, adding that he didn't think I would have too much trouble in getting out once I got home. The CO was surprised at my unorthodox method of getting back to England but there was nothing he could do. The journey home was most luxurious and very interesting; all fixed up with the help of the Kahlid. Overland from Khartoum to Asmara by train, I travelled for about two days and nights in a most comfortable style with good service and excellent food. At the rail-end I trans-shipped to a Nile paddle steamer and spent a very relaxed few days in great comfort gently cruising down the Nile. The scenery, the sight of the other boats plying this waterway, and the beautiful sunsets had to be seen to be believed.

It is not surprising that this trip has now become a great tourist attraction costing £1,000 and more – all the more satisfying as far as I was concerned, having a free ride.

The only trouble was that there was a mad woman aboard. She was small, thickly set, oldish and witchlike with long white hair. She made a perfect nuisance of herself by coming up to talk to people and perpetually making a scene and complaining. When on her own she would mutter and talk to herself. All the passengers were scared of her, and rightly so because at the end of the trip she became violent and was locked up. The last I saw of this strange woman was at the start of the final train journey to Cairo. She was put aboard a special compartment in a straitjacket with two white coated attendants.

I continued my leisurely journey home by boat from Port Said. I felt I might as well take full benefit and reward for my services – any future excursion of this sort would have to be paid out of my own pocket. The Company Commander course at Warminster did not prove too difficult or energetic – in fact I, with quite a string of medals by this time, was much in demand

and often asked to express my views, based on my experience in various wartime situations. Most of the students were very young fellows or junior staff officers who had not seen overseas service.

With my wife and daughter I was billeted at a nice pub in the High Street and afterwards at a comfortable guest house just outside the town. The child was carted around everywhere in a carry cot and was often left in the back seat of my old car in the cot while we went out to dinner. Sometimes we were accused of being callous, but the baby thrived and became accustomed to this nomadic life. I passed out of the course with flying colours and was invited to become an instructor – but I had other thoughts on my mind and was busy trying to extricate myself from the clutches of the Service. I was given indefinite leave pending my release and went to stay at my wife's home in Scotland.

It was springtime which coincided with the period when my father-in-law had taken a salmon beat on the Dee, further north. The fishing party was accommodated in the annexe of a nice hotel near the river and fished every day for a fortnight with considerable success – the best day yielding nine fish to my own rod. By an extraordinary coincidence I learnt that my old friend Diana, with her mother and father, had come to live in a large house on the edge of the river right in the middle of the beat I was fishing on. This was an unexpected bonus and I immediately went to pay her a visit.

After the death of her husband in a flying accident she had remarried, but this evidently did not last long. Although still married they were living apart. My wife considered fishing to be a terrible bore and was not in the slightest bit interested. She only appeared at the main fishing hut at lunch time – indeed she brought the lunch down from the hotel; the men attended to their own requirements so far as the booze was concerned. Dot's involvement with the fishing was entirely social. On the other hand Diana was a great sporting lady and a very good fisherman, so most days we met on the river bank. With her local knowledge she was helpful in explaining the lies and the likely places to catch a salmon and on a number of occasions in difficult water she gaffed a fish for me.

Usually after dinner at the hotel some rods would go out and fish until it got dark. There was always a favourite time and that was when the woodcock was flighting across the river at dusk, more often than not a fisherman would get a pull then; but it was rare to land more than one or two fish during an evening's fishing. Sometimes I would make an arrangement with Diana to meet well upstream for an evening's fishing. It was helpful having Diana around because the daytime ghillies knocked off at about five pm and together we sometimes accounted for the odd fish; whether or not anything was caught we at least spent some agreeable times together.

Soon after this fishing holiday Diana's parents bought another fine house further downstream with its own fishing, where she worked as a ghillie-cum-gardener. It was not until many years later that, travelling round the north, on my own and fishing here and there, I went to stay with Diana. She was still doing the same thing and had accounted for a great number of salmon in the intervening years.

Finally, word came through that this most irregular Regular Soldier had got his release from the Army. So it was back to square one: no job, no prospects and little in the way of qualifications. It was not that I had been totally idle during the last few months. I had put together some family property and started farming in a gentlemanly way. This enterprise proved to be quite successful – not particularly by my own endeavours but, through my Army training, in selecting the right man to do the job. I and the manager, a practical man yet well versed in modern farming techniques, got on like a house on fire – each contributing a little bit of knowledge to the other. From small beginnings the acreage expanded until some years later we had developed a first class property which was making quite a good profit.

Probably the secret of my success in this sphere was my reluctance to borrow money. Any profit was ploughed back into the business to enable me to expand my various enterprises, buying new machinery and so forth. While this is a great philosophy if you have any money to start with, I had none. The choice was forced upon me; I must land a job with good prospects and the farm would look after itself. In any event, I felt that I had something to offer if only I could find the right niche; after all I was still only twenty-eight years old and eager and willing to work hard provided I could see some light at the end of the tunnel.

I again found myself in Scotland staying with my in-laws, racking my brain as to what course I should adopt. One day it became as clear as a crystal. I smelt Scotch whisky in the air – why not become a Scotch Whisky distiller? After all, farming and Scotch are not all that far apart. I knew how to grow barley, and malted barley was the main ingredient of good Scotch whisky. Now the adrenalin was flowing. I wasted no time in composing a letter to the Scottish office of one of the most famous Scotch Whisky companies in the world, mentioning that I was very keen to join them in whatever capacity they felt I might be of use to them; mentioning furthermore that I would be happy to work for nothing until I had proved myself.

The letter, for some reason or another, surprised the Scottish office and the director in charge there decided to send the application on to the managing director in London with the good news that he would be pleased to see me for an interview whenever it was convenient. It transpired that John Barr Cumming, the managing director, although getting on in years had been a gallant soldier in the Great War and had been badly wounded. Evidently my letter, giving some details of my career to date including particulars of my war service, struck the right chord.

The interview took place in a delightful old building in the West End – the whole place seemed to me to have style written all over it. I was conducted upstairs by a commissionaire and handed over to Gladys Young, the managing director's secretary – many years later to become my own secretary. Gladys, a dear person, produced a cup of tea and advised me to be myself and try to regard the boss as a benevolent old uncle. I was duly ushered in and we sat down and talked. There was no barrier or difficulty whatsoever. Our conversation ranged over the beauty of Scotland, salmon fishing, stalking and shooting and I was pleased to find that we had a few Scottish friends in common. The managing director in turn gave me a run down of the Scottish whisky distilling world and what it was all about.

It seemed to me that the time had arrived for a little action on my part, so I said to him: 'Are you going to have me?'

He replied: 'Yes, I'll take you – when do you want to come, and incidentally when I wrote I asked you to bring a testimonial, have you got it?'

I said that I hadn't got one yet but hoped to produce one within the next week or so. Then it came to the date of joining the organization. In a month's time it would be around mid-August – the managing director pondered a while and then came out with the comment that the 12th would be no use – presumably I would be grouse shooting then. I had fixed up a delayed honeymoon at Lugarno, Switzerland, and had no wish to disturb this arrangement. I would be returning mid-September. This information was passed to the managing director and he was most sympathetic and remarked: 'Have a good holiday. It will be that last decent one you will get for quite a long time'.

The testimonial from my Commanding Officer eventually arrived on the managing director's desk. It read as follows:

'Major Ripley was a gallant soldier. He is a good boxer and a good shot and he has a happy knack of achieving maximum results with a minimum amount of effort.'

And so, with this somewhat dubious testimonial, I embarked on my new career as a Scotch Whisky distiller.

11

The Art of Distilling

On Monday morning in early September, 1947, I duly reported for work at 63 St James's Street, the head office of John Walker & Son Ltd, the eminent Scotch Whisky firm. I was a little apprehensive but well pleased with myself for securing a job in this well-known international company.

I had no idea what was in store and in fact I only had a sketchy knowledge of business procedure. Although I was taken on as a 'trainee', the usual six months probationary period applied. I was quite determined to learn as much as I could in the shortest possible time; and I hoped to have a certain amount of fun and enjoyment while being put through the mill. In truth it was essential for me to apply myself and succeed for I had no money and wife and a daughter. Moreover I liked the style and affluence of the various company directors I had met and felt this would be a good target to aim at.

I spent the first few days hovering around the office with a guide introducing me to the staff and the various departments. I was based on the home trade order department where two old-timers called Jim and Gerald were the stalwarts. Gerald had a great capacity for beer and he could be more or less written off after the lunch-time break. If he failed to get his fill in the local pubs he could generally be found in Leslie's entertainment room. At that time Leslie had a most unusual job: from his well-stocked cupboard he would entertain visitors with drams all day starting at about nine thirty am and always having one himself. All manner of people came into Leslie's reception room – 'refreshment room' would have been a better name – and they came from all walks of life: from publicans and customers to most of the tradespeople in St James's.

The local gunsmith was a very regular visitor; he and Leslie pent many hours together on most days of the week. It was virtually an open house. The thinking behind this generosity was that Walkers had to be seen to be hospitable: if treated well those who were refreshed would stock up with the product in their own homes or nominate the brand when visiting a pub. Many customers in the London area would come to the office to pay their accounts personally in the knowledge that they would spend a happy hour or two with Leslie afterwards. It was estimated that Leslie's consumption was in the order of two or three bottles a day. Yet he never had a glass in front of him when he was on his own – it would be considered impolite when a visitor arrived and, besides, a director might walk in. An unfinished glass of whisky would be deposited in the top right-hand drawer of his desk and he would only retrieve it when with friends. Leslie was a convivial fellow and would always help himself to another drink when the next visitor came in.

I became his friend early on and spent many happy hours with him. He was a good source of information about the firm and there was little he did not know about the directors and staff. Furthermore he had the key of the sample room and together we would go to 'nose' the whiskies sent down daily from Scotland after the directors' inspection. Leslie reached retirement age but sadly did not live long afterwards.

As to work in the home trade order department, this was straightforward and rather boring. Customers were all restricted to quotas based on their pre-war purchases. Invariably they wanted more than they got and sometimes they were accommodated by a few extra cases from a small reserve stock. Winston Churchill, then leader of the Opposition, was one of the people who benefited from this reserve. He was always a staunch supporter of Black Label, indeed he painted a nice picture of a bottle of Black Label beside his other favourite tipples, a bottle of Hine Brandy and a bottle of Pol Roger Champagne. Later on I tried to acquire this picture for the firm, but was unsuccessful. Churchill's order was always put through by telephone from his suppliers, Hatch Mansfield. The dialogue went as follows: 'The gentleman requires x cases of Black Label at the usual address'.

Jim, the head of the department, had been dealing with this particular order for many years and knew exactly what to do. A special delivery would be made the next day. But one day Jim was away from his office when the message came through over the telephone and a newcomer answered it. The message was the same as usual and the fellow replied: 'Who's this 'ere *gentleman* you're talking about and what's the *bleedin address*?' The Hatch Mansfield man said: 'Find out', and put down the telephone. On hearing about the message on his return to the office Jim had the whisky despatched straight away. In future he made sure that everyone in his department understood this respectful and unusual form of ordering whisky from John Walker.

After my initiation in the London office I was called for one day by the managing director who told me that I was to be sent up to Scotland for a year or so to learn the fundamentals of blending and the manufacture of Scotch whisky. The managing director who was to be my tutor and mentor in this important art was John Barr-Cumming, a benevolent and kindly Scot. His family had been owners of the famous Mortlach Distillery on Speyside since the illicit distilling days. The distillery was acquired by John Walker & Sons in the 1920s. They soon realized that they had made a particularly good purchase in getting John Barr thrown in with the deal. He was steeped in the tradition of Scotch whisky and was an acknowledged expert in this field.

His instructions to me were that I was to learn everything I possibly could during my sojourn in Scotland, both at the large blending and bottling establishment in Kilmarnock and during an extended course at various distilleries in the Highlands. Furthermore, John Barr expected regular communications from me to let him know how I was getting on. This agreement carried on until John Barr's untimely death in 1950. He would always answer my letter meticulously explaining in detail any misconceptions I had formed, or explaining and simplifying any points that I found difficult to grasp.

John Barr was a short, stocky man with a clipped military moustache. His head was tilted to one side which gave the impression that it was resting on his shoulder. In fact he had been severely wounded in the 1914-18 War and he was always in great pain. To alleviate this discomfort – or perhaps because he had been weaned on Scotch whisky – he consumed large quantities of the product starting at an early hour. It was estimated that he was over a bottle-a-day man, but he showed no sign whatsoever of inebriation.

As a base for me and my wife and small daughter, Caroline, and a young nanny I took a year's lease on a sturdy house on the South beach of Troon on the Aryshire coast. In good visibility there was a beautiful seascape with Arran clearly discernible due west and the rocky isle of Ailsa Craig, famous for curling stones, further south. It was a healthy spot but the prevailing wind from the sea became very tiresome. No large trees could survive the gale. What trees there were, round the sea side, were stunted and bent nearly horizontal. When the wind was at its worst it was difficult to get into the front door of the house and on quite a few occasions I was obliged – while reasonably sober – to go down on all fours to get in.

Golf courses abounded in the area and the famous Old Troon links was a mere two minutes walk away. There was a convenient little branch line from Troon to Kilmarnock (now, of course, disbanded) so I travelled to work daily on the train, which was rarely full. In the winter months I would often arrive home wet through after the half-mile walk from the station. Umbrellas were useless against the wind; they collapsed and turned inside out.

This pleasant enough mode of life only lasted for a brief spell because arrangements had been made for the beginning of my working and educational course at the Highland Distillers. My first tour of duty was at Elgin Distillery, living at the Gordon Arms Hotel, Elgin, where I stayed about a month before moving on to Cardhu Distillery where I was housed in a workman's cottage. This was a fascinating and rewarding time with some hard physical work thrown in. Every co-operation was given by the distillery managers and the work people. The latter had grown up in the industry as indeed had their fathers and grandfathers. They were loyal and dedicated people yet they did not always know why their efforts produced such delectable Scotch whisky – it was up to us to try to find the secret.

The two other trainees and myself now working and gaining knowledge at Linkwood Distillery did all the jobs of unloading sacks of barley to storage of the finished product in the bonded warehouse. 'Happy', later to become one of the leading lights in the distillery world, was my particular companion. I pleaded a weak back so Happy and the other trainee, David, were persuaded to shoulder the heavy sacks of barley to the malting floor.

John Barr-Cumming, besides keeping in regular communication from London, indicated that he expected to receive a treatise about the manufacture of Scotch whisky at the end of the course. I duly made copious notes and sought information from distillery managers, stillmen, mashturn men and excisemen for my *magnum opus*.

On returning to the Johnnie Walker headquarters at Kilmarnock, full of enthusiasm about the making of Scotch whisky at both malt and grain distilleries, I was put into the blending department. Here I had a great opportunity of tasting and, with the assistance of C.V. Smith, the production director, and Bill Fulton, getting to know the various single whiskies, both new and matured. Fortunately I was endowed with a good-sized nose and a very sensitive sense of smell.

All whiskies have their individual characteristics. On a blind tasting, sampling about forty different single whiskies, I invariably identified more than ninety per cent correctly. With practice and a sensitive nose the tasting developed into a memory test. So far as new whiskies were concerned the blender liked to check that the whisky was all right for laying down, and for ultimate use in blending. With regard to the matured whiskies, all the great whisky houses have a recipe. In the case of Johnnie Walker over forty single whiskies are put into the blend so it is important that the product from individual distilleries is consistent. Besides there are times – particularly at the end of the Second World War – when shortages occur and one of the ingredients of the blend has to be substituted. This requires professional knowledge of the blender in order to ensure that the finished product – the stuff in the bottle – never varies.

It was now time to move on to the bond bulk warehouse, which was all under bond and indeed under the close security of the Customs and Excise officers. David, a Scot, later to become secretary of the company and a director, was in charge of this operation aided by myself and another junior. We were housed in a glass box not much bigger than a telephone kiosk with a one bar electric heater to keep out the elements in the winter and it was a very cold place indeed, but at least it was a pleasant temperature during the hot summer months. During the winter I usually wore a thick tweed suit, especially favouring a green lovat mixture. One bitterly cold day I got too close to the miserable heating apparatus and went up in flames. My leg was scorched but at least the Lovat suit was not a total write off. A local tailor put on a large patch on one of the trouser legs of approximately the right colour and the faithful suiting did yeoman service for many years afterwards.

Breaking down high proof blended whisky before bottling was one of the more responsible and tricky tasks we had to undertake. Vats containing more than twenty thousand gallons of blended whisky, all over-proof and of varying strengths, had to be reduced in strength by the addition of water to the bottling requirements – for example seventy proof (thirty under proof) for the UK and eighty-five proof for the USA and some other countries. We worked out our calculations on a slide-rule based on a formula that had been handed down by our predecessors. Should we dilute the whisky too much there would be very severe repercussions and the guilty party would be called before the director in charge and more likely than not given his marching orders.

From my minuscule office we could observe the excisemen in their infinitely superior quarters. These officers had their books to keep and it was necessary to have a close liaison. Most of the time they would be testing the strength – by means of a hydrometer and thermometer in a sample glass – of the various casks and vats before and after an operation and then record their findings. Some officers were more generous than others and over a period could save the trader in duty or allowances many thousands of pounds.

Big Mac was the opposite variety. He was a scholarly Highlander and a man of very few words. He invariably wore a plus-four Lovat suit and so far as he was concerned the Customs and Excise men were his lords and masters, and he would never depart one iota from his book of rules and regulations. He was a mathematician and always correct in his calculations. Although fair he was never known to favour the trading company.

Algy Yellan was another of the excisemen: a big bluff fellow with a great sense of humour and fun and always ready for a good laugh. He was a friend of everyone including myself and all the others who worked in the bond bulk. He knew his job completely and made light of it. There were always occasions when, whilst sticking to the book, a little 'tolerance' (a technical word) could be allowed. Unlike Big Mac, Algy would tend to come down in favour of the trading company. On his retirement Algy was taken on by the company as a visitors' guide round the works with additional public relations duties. He completed a number of happy years in this role.

Bill was the third officer in the Customs and Excise who put in a regular appearance. He was a thin, jumpy sort of fellow who looked rather like a weasel. There was no doubt that he knew his job very well but he became addicted to the product and would tipple considerable quantities from the sample glass he was supposed to be testing. The company boys could see the signs and often had a bet as to whether he would turn up the next day. On these occasions it was generally thought that he would fill his ample briefcase with sample bottles of over-proof whisky for a continuing binge at his home. More often than not he would be away for about a week and return as if nothing had happened until his next bout. It was said that his wife, aware of his weakness with booze, would not allow any drink in the house. Evidently he had a good supply in the garden shed and he would disappear there all day under the pretext of potting plants.

As was to happen a number of times in my career, I assumed unexpected responsibility for the bond bulk as David, the young boss, was promoted to the secretarial side of the business. At this time I was also putting the finishing touches to my treatise on the making of Highland malt whisky and grain whisky. John Barr-Cumming, the managing director, was very pleased with this work and he wrote a nice letter congratulating me on my grasp of the distilling process and for the time and trouble I had taken in preparing this detailed and lucid paper. At that time very few manuals on distilling had been published and they were very hard to come by. So my contribution was much sought after, particularly by a succession of students who were sent off by their various companies on subsequent distillery courses.

Although still pretty junior in the organization, I was quite happy to return to the head office at 63 St James's Street now that I was in a position to talk with some authority on the manufacture of Scotch Whisky. Indeed I was one of the few in the firm, including most of the directors, who had been given the opportunity of learning all about distilling at the grass roots. While this background training proved to be useful later on I was not called upon to put my knowledge to any useful purpose for some years. Yet socially it was an asset. Friends and acquaintances when they learnt that I worked for a famous Scotch whisky company seemed at that time to have many questions to ask. The stuff was still in short supply after the war years and it was always a newsworthy subject. I was pleased to answer any queries and expand on the mystique. Indeed I was flattered by the attention and was already beginning to consider myself an expert after barely two years in the business.

I was soon to be brought down to earth. Whether the bosses did not know what to do with me or whether they thought the time had arrived for me to widen my experience I never discovered. I found myself in the export invoice department. This called for a good knowledge of maths – a subject at which I had never excelled. Fortunately I had a good tutor in Charlie, head of the department and an old servant of the company, who had a wide experience in the export business and was very patient. There were three other excellent ladies in the department: the Misses Prickett, Judd and Farmer, who did the typing and a certain amount of figure work. What I particularly remember are the number of copies of each invoice – 'flimsies' as they were known – usually comprising six or more copies made of air mail type material.

It was important for Charlie and now me to get the sums right first time because it was extremely difficult to alter the copies. Furthermore, being the junior, I had the task of taking the documents each evening to a director for signature. One director – who perhaps had better remain nameless – was a pigheaded sort of blighter who had no knowledge whatsoever of price or rates of exchange. If there was any sort of alteration in the invoice and copies, although they were perfectly clear and readable, they would be sent back for retyping and this generally involved working late.

All the time I was beginning to master the arithmetic and indeed later on in my career I came to be considered numerate. This goes to show that a bad maths report at school is not disastrous and in fact means little. For speed in calculations

Charlie taught his number two to work in decimals of a pound – this, of course, was in the old days of pounds, shillings and pence. This proved to be most effective, accurate and speedy. Alas Charlie, my mentor and friend, was transferred to another job in the export field so I assumed responsibility for the department while still something of a greenhorn. Fortunately Charlie was still in the same room – an enormous area with a minstrels gallery which at one time had been a ball room for a well known West End club. I often sought his advice on tricky problems.

To compound my difficulties the pound was devalued overnight against the American dollar. This had the effect of altering all prices in America, Latin America and many other places. The immediate reaction from customers and agents abroad was to demand immediate 'Proforma' invoices giving the 'CIF' (cost, insurance, freight) price to the port of destination.

Telegrams, telexes and letters came piling in which entailed working all hours. It was seldom that I finished work until ten in the evening. Even once things had quietened down the little department was grossly overworked and it was unusual for us to get away before seven pm. The three girls should have had a special medal struck for them: they never complained and never received any extra money for overtime. What a change from today when the department is three or four times as large and regular hours are adhered to, or overtime paid. Although the volume of business had increased four-fold the documentation is more or less unchanged. The thing that amazed me in the late 1940s was that practically every consignment sent abroad was paid for before it was shipped – a good prudent Scottish way of doing business.

I clearly required an assistant and it took some time to get one. Eventually Ivor, a delightful young ex-Guards officer, joined me. Although he was very willing and tried his hardest this trainee was a square peg in a round hole. He became a true friend but was of little help in the department. Yet somehow we managed to survive with the girls doing that bit extra to help us out. One day Ivor confided in me that he was not cut out for business; in fact he hated it. Books were his line of country. He decided to give in his notice. We met up from time to time afterwards but it was not until some months had gone by that I learnt that Ivor was doing social work in the East End and that he was far from well. All along, it seemed, he had been suffering from leukaemia and he knew his days were numbered. He died within the year.

Ivor's mother, a most charming person, subsequently told me all this and thanked me very much for making his life tolerable towards the end. Ivor never complained or divulged his illness. He was a brave man.

12

On The Road

In 1950 my old friend John Barr Cumming, the managing director, died. There was much speculation as to who would take over from him. The most likely choice seemed to be one of the directors of the export department, but the choice went to Harry Braid, son of the famous golfer James Braid. He was a huge fellow – at least six feet three inches – and, needless to say, a scratch golfer. Harry had been secretary of the company for a few years and was very well liked by everyone for his compassion and kindness. It could truly be said of Harry that he was one of the world's gentlemen – a tribute that is not lightly given to anyone.

Old James Braid, the 'pro' at Walton Heath Golf Club and winner of all the major golf tournaments – he won the Open a few times – was a friend of Sir Alexander Walker. They played golf together at Troon and no doubt old James would give Sir Alexander a few tips to improve his game. As a result of this friendship the two young Braids joined the firm before the war. James, the younger brother, no mean golfer himself, became a director in Scotland whilst Harry took over as managing director in London.

If Harry had decided to follow in his father's footsteps there is no doubt that he would have become a successful professional. Curiously, when he started to play at a tender age at Elie golf course, Fife, he was left-handed. Old Braid, realizing that his boy had potential, would have none of this and made Harry switch to playing right-handed. In spite of this he became one of the best amateurs in the country with a plus handicap. He was christened Harry *Muirfield* Braid because his father laid out that renowned championship course in Scotland.

Scotch whisky was still on quota in the home trade in 1950 and was to remain so for some years ahead. The directors felt that some form of sales representation should be set up against the time when whisky became in free supply. The large sales force was abandoned at the start of the war so there had been practically no personal contact with customers throughout the UK for the past ten years. I was surprised one morning to be summoned from my export desk to the managing director's office, where the other home trade directors and executives were assembled. I was told of their plan of action, namely that a skeleton sales force was to be set up and that I had been selected to cover the Midlands, including Birmingham, Wales and the West Country. There were two other appointments in England. Jack was to do the South, the Home Counties and East Anglia; Duncan was given the North of England. Similarly there were a couple of appointments in Scotland.

Both Jack and Duncan had been in the firm in pre-war days so they had some idea of what might be expected of them. I had none, but I felt it might be quite entertaining and with luck I should get a day's hunting a week, with some shooting and fishing thrown in. My first task was to find somewhere to live. It was suggested that I should go to Birmingham – the most important place in my area so far as business was concerned. After a lot of searching we found an agreeable property in Warwickshire: the Hey House, Lapworth, with about six acres, a mature orchard and a pretty garden. In fact I had little to do with this acquisition. My wife, with her family, made the final decision which was fair enough since she was to pay for the house.

For my part, I would have been perfectly happy to live in an old stone house near Craven Arms, Shropshire, which was left to my family by an aunt. But my wife hated that part of the world and would have nothing to do with it. The job entailed being away a great deal unless I was working in Birmingham or in the local area. More often than not I would set off on Monday and return on Friday. The head office had a pretty good idea where I was all the time. I had more or less a set route, having sent call cards the week before. I was expected to make a certain number of calls each day sending back the written up journey cards at regular intervals.

For the first year or so I travelled by train, bus or hitched lifts. Cars were scarce and it was impossible to get new ones, even for such a small sales force. Looking back, the old firm were extraordinarily mean and inconsiderate about this: they should, of course, have bought good secondhand cars for their people – at whatever price. Walkers were not exactly on the bread line. We did have a little family car which I used sometimes, but more often than not it was required for school runs.

After a year's travelling – which is not greatly to be recommended, although it had its lighter moments and it was always interesting to discover new parts of the country – I was told to collect an old Morris from the garage in London. This was a sturdy pre-war banger known as FUF (the car number) and the speedo reading was not far off 100,000 miles. Yet it did me well enough and, apart from bad brakes and uneven steering, it chugged along nicely. The only troubles ever encountered were punctures and these were frequent – usually in inhospitable countryside such as the Welsh mountains or Dartmoor.

A fishing rod and golf clubs were always stowed away in the car and my daily journeys were organized so that I usually ended up at an hotel with fishing or a golf course nearby. The trade were interested to see whisky travellers around again and, on the whole, they were hospitable, particularly the country brewers. One such brewer had his office in Plymouth and on the floor alongside him he kept a crate of Tivvy beer. I would arrive at about eleven am and together we would dispose of the bottles. Having got the taste, we would visit some of Peter's pubs and consume more Tivvy before settling down to a late and extended lunch at one of his hostelries. Later we would return to the office to pack up and have a dram or two before going home to Peter's house on Dartmoor. Usually I would take Peter and Joan, his wife, out to dinner at some country restaurant, returning to spend the night at his attractive and comfortable farmhouse.

The next day I might go on to the brewery head office in Bridgwater where I would again receive a warm welcome. The managing director, Mickie, shared a small Dickensian room with his colleague, the company secretary and director. They worked standing at a high desk facing each other. Mickie's side was piled high with five or six columns of paper, whereas the secretary's side of the desk was quite clear. On arrival I would be ushered in by a clerk who was told to go straight away to produce a bottle of Black Label and three glasses. This call entailed finishing the bottle before we went out to lunch together. Rather intrigued by their business methods, I asked Mickie why he had all the papers stacked in front of him while there were none the other side. 'That's simple,' he said. 'He does the work and I do the filing.'

To prove the point and the efficiency of his system he got his colleague to ask for a letter dated some time back. Mickie immediately went to one of the columns and extracted the letter about three parts down the pile. He handed it over the desk with a happy and contented smile.

Whisky and wine representatives are in rather a special category – probably because of the well-being engendered by the products they purvey. More often than not we would discuss trade topics over a glass of something or other. It should be born in mind that this was long before breathalyser days. Nevertheless caution and tact were often necessary. The same applied to the clothes you wore. In the big towns and cities I would wear an ordinary business suit; in the country parts I would wear tweeds; in the real bush areas I sometimes felt more comfortable, and well received, in my shooting clothes. Or, when visiting customers at the seaside resorts, I might wear a blazer and slacks.

On one trip to the West Country dressed in this way I decided on the spur of the moment to visit the Scilly Isles. I took FUF to St Just airport, stuffed a pair of bathing trunks into my pocket and caught the little aeroplane to St Mary's. I made my one call there and decided to visit the one and only pub of Tresco. A fisherman obliged by taking me there and promised to get me back again to St Mary's to catch the plane. The call completed, with a little lunch and a few drams, I set off for a beautiful sandy beach for a swim and some sunbathing. Apart from the shock of getting into the sea – the water is bitterly cold round the islands – I spent a happy few hours dozing, entirely on my own, under a beautiful cloudless sky. As good as his word, the fisherman tooted and came on to the beach to collect me and I duly caught the plane back to the mainland. Travelling had its compensations, particularly when all charges are picked up by the firm!

Fortunately there were quite a number of humorous incidents that made this mode of life entertaining, if sometimes embarrassing. One such occasion occurred when I called on the wine and spirit manager of a brewery in Somerset (now defunct). The directors were good friends and I had learnt that the manager – who after all did the buying – took umbrage and was jealous because he had never received a visit. On entering his den, which was a combined office and sample room, I was surprised to see a thin red-faced man with his large nose embedded into a sherry sampling glass. The sherry was bubbling away and the man appeared to be in severe distress. This was too much for me: I broke into peals of laughter and had to leave the room – not a very auspicious introduction. On returning to the room, I was quite unable to carry on any coherent conversation.

Some months later another representative took over this area and the buyer asked what had happened to me, indicating that he presumed I had been fired and was no longer with the firm. It was discovered later on that the wine and spirit manager was quite a serious toper. He duly received the order of the boot for over-indulgence.

Going round Bedford with another colleague, I was warned that the wine and spirit proprietor had a strange affliction. After every sentence he grunted like a pig. Again, I found that it was quite impossible to keep a straight face when these porcined snufflings were emitted and once more had to leave the room on some pretext, convulsed in mirth.

A journey round the Rhondda Valley, culminating in Rumney, just north of Cardiff, where some large breweries were situated, was always entertaining and rather awe-inspiring. The brewery wine and spirit managers were usually descended from coal mining stock and were great sportsmen. Early in the war I had commanded a platoon of coal miners so I was quite at home with them. Trout fishing was the usual topic of conversation and there was not a river they did not know for many miles around. Many useful hints and locations were given – practically all on private water. Poaching is rife in Wales and, evidently, so far as they were concerned, added zest to the sport.

When visiting the managing director at a brewery in the middle of Abertillery, quite a large town at the top of the

Rhondda Valley, my mind was completely taken off the subject we were discussing over a glass of whisky by the noise of sheep bleating just outside the boardroom window. Rather apprehensive, and feeling that the demon drink had at last caught up with me, I asked the managing director if he had heard the sheep. He assured me there was nothing to worry about. The sheep came down from the mountains and wandered all round the town, upsetting the dustbins in their scavenging.

One hot summer afternoon, after a good lunch in Plymouth, I called on a stuffy old brewery. I had been kept waiting for about half an hour in the reception room and nodded off into a deep sleep. Evidently my loud snores reminded the wine and spirit manager of my presence. I was awoken by a tap on the shoulder and a suggestion that I might find it more comfortable in my bed back at the hotel.

Before Gordon took over my area I was showing him around Porthcawl and, a martyr to dyspepsia, he was gobbling a quantity of Rennies indigestion tablets. I was offered one and chewed it before making a call at a wine and spirit shop. I noticed that the manager kept looking at me in a strange way and that Gordon was trying his hardest to stifle a bad attack of giggles. On leaving the premises I asked what on earth was going on. Gordon suggested that I should have a look at myself in a mirror. Not accustomed to eating the tablets, my lips had turned white. I looked more like a circus clown than the representative of an important Scotch whisky company.

One day I received a message from Smithy, the home trade director of Johnnie Walker, that I was to meet him at the Bell Hotel, Gloucester, so that we could travel together to visit customers in South Wales. We duly met at about eleven thirty in the morning. Smithy had driven up in his large eight-cylinder Lagonda – a fine motor car. On arrival the boot of the car was opened up. This contained a clutch of custom-built suitcases which were taken away by a porter. There was also a large built-in mahogany drink cabinet stuffed full of Johnnie Walker Red Label bottles and half-bottles. This was duly opened and I was instructed to take a load up to Smithy's bedroom.

Before any unpacking was done, Smithy headed straight for the bar where large Johnnie Walkers were ordered immediately. Next Smithy said: 'We must make some calls. We must not waste a minute.' We set off down the High Street stopping at any promising looking hostelries and taking a large snort at each one. Woe betide me if the product was not on optic at any of the places we visited. We returned to the Bell for a late lunch with the usual bottle of Red Label on the table.

After a robust repast and a lot of whisky I was heading towards my bedroom to sleep it off when there was a shout from the other end of the corridor intimating that I was to collect my tooth glass and report to Smithy's room. A strong afternoon session was suddenly interrupted by Smithy exclaiming that it was five thirty pm and that the hotel bar was open. A few large ones were immediately attended to and then we resumed our excursion of the morning, visiting various pubs. On returning to the hotel for dinner – needless to say – we made a lengthy stop at the bar. By this stage the barman had developed into a proper friend. We dined well, with the usual bottle on the table, then came a further visit to the bar and another heavy session in Smithy's bedroom under the pretence of a night cap before turning in.

Orders were given for an early call and after breakfast the next morning we set forth in the Lagonda for South Wales. Smithy, an ex-Flying Corps and RAF man, enjoyed speed and we proceeded at a great pace with a lot of noise. At one point, close to Newport, the speedo registered one hundred miles per hour. Eventually the car coughed and spluttered to a stop at a garage close to the Royal Hotel, Cardiff, where we were staying. Evidently something was burnt and a replacement had to be sent from London.

Calls were made to brewers and wine and spirit merchants round the city interspersed with frequent visits to pubs. Smithy had a remarkable constitution: he got up early in the morning and never seemed to suffer from a hangover. He smoked like a chimney and would drink anything that was put in front of him; but his favourite tipple remained Red Label. He was probably getting on towards sixty where I was then about thirty-five. He was a tall, well-built fellow with a good mop of greying hair and a florid face. He had been born at Timaru Creek in the South Island, New Zealand, and came over with his fellow Kiwis to fight in the First War. Smithy flew one of the early biplane fighters in France and had some hair-raising stories to tell. At the end he was shot down but managed to get out of the plane unscathed – fortunately on the right side of the line.

After that war he married into a rich brewing family and became a great socialite in London. He was a friend of the Prince of Wales and Lord Brownlow, spending holidays on country estates or in the South of France. Smithy was an arrogant sort of fellow. He was always very well dressed and he could be most affable – until the demon drink got hold of him. Then he had a vile temper and a little tuft of hair on his red nose would stand up on end. This was the time to beware. Invariably at a smart restaurant, such as the Savoy, he would have a complaint – usually aggravated by a heavy session at the bar beforehand. The wine was never right. It was either the wrong temperature or in his opinion 'corked'. He would make a tremendous fuss. Replacement bottles were always provided with apologies, probably because he tipped on a lavish scale.

Following the usual pattern, the first evening at the Royal in Cardiff was much the same as that spent at the Bell in Gloucester. There was, however, one big difference: a mix-up had occurred in the booking and only one double room had been reserved. All the rest were occupied. Smithy told me to get my bag and that we would share the same room. What remained of the booze left in the boot of the Lagonda was brought up to the bedroom, save for a few half bottles which were to be handed out as gifts – not least to the garage mechanics who were effecting repairs to the car.

Quite an enjoyable evening was spent together, with a good dinner at the hotel and the accustomed routine afterwards. At about midnight, though, it was found necessary to call on the resources of the night porter as we had exhausted supplies in the bedroom. The Smithy warning signs were now beginning to manifest themselves. The blood vessels on his forehead were starting to protrude and the face was becoming redder than usual. But, more sinisterly, the hairs on his nose were now standing straight upright. He suddenly shouted at me: 'Why the hell did you join Johnnie Walker – you are no bloody good at all'.

A little taken aback, I thought to myself that he might be my boss but I was not standing for this sort of treatment. 'And who the hell do you think you are?' I replied. 'A blasted New

Zealander from Timaru Creek, with bad manners and a bad temper. And you drink too much.'

Smithy fumed and spluttered and reached for the bottle which he emptied. Not content to call it a day, he stormed out of the room. I followed in a few minutes and found him in the night porter's cubby-hole having a brisk exchange with the unfortunate man because he had run out of whisky. Smithy then switched to brandy. Eventually we got to bed, though still hurling invective at each other. I was a little apprehensive that I might have gone a bit too far. But at seven am I was woken up by a remarkably hearty Smithy. For my part I was suffering from an appalling hangover. I pulled the bedclothes over my head, hoping to have another hour or two's kip. Not a bit of it. Smithy pulled the bedclothes back and yanked me out of bed, telling me that it was a lovely day and that we still had a lot of work to do.

Smithy's recuperative powers were extraordinary. Furthermore, he never referred to the previous night's row; it was quite probable that he had a black-out and had no recollection of the incident. At any rate, we were good pals again and set off after breakfast in the Lagonda, travelling at great speed up the valleys visiting breweries and various other outlets. It was with some relief that I was returned to Gloucester that day to find my way home.

Unfortunately after his retirement Smithy came to grief with a severe fall down the stairs of the RAF Club. He lost his leg. Yet he was a gallant fellow and a survivor. Later on I used to see him with his artificial leg at the head office in London where he was never known to refuse a little refreshment in the shape of some Red Label. Eventually his liver packed up and he had to make do with ginger ale.

When working for a big firm it is always a good thing to have a second string to your bow. I was fortunate in this respect in that my father handed over a chunk of agricultural property in order to alleviate death duties. The other task I had to fulfil in my spare time was the trusteeship of a family business in Bradford. My great-grandfather had been a rich self-made man. Starting from quite humble origins he became one of the leading woollen textile manufacturers and dyers in that city. The Ripleys started a famous firm called The Bradford Dyers. It was said that one of my forbears took an old pram full of cloth from Huddersfield to Bradford to get it dyed. He was so impressed with the process that he asked to be taken on. That was the start of the family fortunes.

After three years covering the Midlands, Wales and the West Country for Johnnie Walker – more often than not only returning to my home, wife and family in Warwickshire at weekends I was becoming bored with the job. The journey round my parish would take about four months. When it was finished I became more and more despondent at the thought of starting the same old routine all over again. So I decided to write to the managing director and ask for an interview at the head office in London. Harry Braid, being a decent and understanding fellow, wrote back immediately and an appointment was fixed up. Harry was well acquainted with the fact that I had entered the firm through John Barr Cumming as he was the company secretary at the time. He was also aware of the special link between the two of us until John Barr's death in 1950.

At our meeting I explained that I had got to know the customers in my territory pretty well during my three year stint; that I had occasionally helped them out with a little extra whisky over and above their quota; and that I had completed the initial representation job to the best of my ability. I then mentioned that I was beginning to feel stale; and that I had little job satisfaction since I was unable to gauge if I had really done any good because of the continued quota system due to the overall shortage of Scotch whisky supplies.

Harry Braid listened, but seemed to be rather puzzled to know what to do about the problem. 'What had John Barr in mind for you?' he said. I replied that I had no idea. 'What is your ambition?' he asked. 'What sort of job do you yourself want?'

Feeling that I had nothing to lose, I said: 'I should like to be sitting in your chair'. Harry was highly entertained and had a good laugh. None the less, I had made my point, indicating that I was ambitious and keen to go up the ladder – and the sooner the better.

The interview ended in a friendly manner with Harry saying he would look into the matter and would write to me in the near future. Smithy had now retired and his job was taken over by Arthur, the new sales director to whom I was directly responsible. I was summoned again to the head office in St James's Street for a further discussion with Harry and Arthur.

My optimism with regard to future progress in the firm was, however, slightly dented as a result of this meeting. They offered me the job of representative of the London Great Metropolitan area. No-one had performed this task since pre-war days, apart from Arthur who had kept contact with a few of the big buyers and who was known at the leading West end hotels. But, of course, I accepted the job, feeling that there were new pastures and that I might be able to make a name for myself in the capital. Moreover my pay was increased and unlimited expenses were allowed.

The only drawback was that, for some reason best known to themselves, I was still not given a car. As a result my expenditure on taxis was very high even for those days.

This upheaval necessitated a move from Warwickshire to the London area. Although it was indicated that I should live in London to be on the job, I and my wife felt otherwise. After a long search we found a very agreeable property alongside the seventeenth fairway of Wentworth's famous 'Burma Road' golf course in Surrey. This is where our children, Caroline and William, were brought up.

The train journey from Virginia Water to Waterloo was fast and generally efficient so travelling to and fro presented no problem. Sometimes I would take my own car by way of a change. The trip would generally take about one hour from door to door.

13

Up and Down St James's

Johnnie Walker was an old-fashioned firm with fixed ideas. Representatives – no matter where they were – were supposed to work from home. All correspondence, instructions and so forth were sent to their home address. This seemed to me to be pretty stupid so I demanded an office in St James's to do my clerical work since I visited headquarters most days. But my request was turned down.

This irritated me. I refused to be left out on a limb so I decided to take matters into my own hands. The registrar, Francis, a good friend, had a large room on the fourth floor which he shared with his secretary. This room, being nicely out of the way, seemed to me to be an ideal place to set up shop. I organized a desk and literally squatted there for the next three years. Whether Arthur and Harry knew about this they never let on. They still wrote to me at my home address but I had nobbled the postal department to deliver the correspondence upstairs. And, moreover, I acquired a part-time secretary.

The metropolitan work was varied, to say the least: customers, whether they were brewers, wine or spirit merchants, hotels or pubs or night clubs were scattered everywhere. When visiting the less salubrious districts of South-East London, or anywhere else for that matter, I learnt where to find cab ranks. On one such occasion I decided to make calls in the Walworth area, a most undesirable part of London. I took the tube to the Elephant and Castle and hired a cab from the rank. From my account cards I told the Cabbie where to go but, having toured around for an hour or two making calls on dilapidated pubs, I could detect that the cabbie was getting pretty fed up. Equally I knew that our friend could do nothing about it because I had not paid the fare and the meter was now registering a sizeable sum. Having emerged from a particularly nasty pub in a most undesirable area, where cabs are an uncommon sight, I was confronted by the cabbie who had been waiting outside the boozer for about half an hour.

'Look 'ere Guv'nor, when are we going home?' he said. 'This ain't cab country.' I took pity on the poor fellow and we returned to the Elephant and Castle tube station where he was paid off with a good tip on top.

On another occasion I took a train to Wimbledon where I went up to the leading cabbie on the rank. I gave him a fistful of call cards asking him to sort them out so as to make a convenient round journey, making sure that he kept Powells of Wimbledon – a very sticky call – as the last port of call.

'I know the trip, Guv'nor,' said the cabbie. 'A bloke got in the cab yesterday and handed me a lot of cards just the same as you. Only this time I am not hanging on at Powells. This bloke kept me waiting two hours there and he weren't too good on his pins when he got into the cab.'

The next day I met Bill Stirling at my club. He was at that time the rep for Buchanans and he turned out to be 'the bloke' who had adopted exactly the same procedure when making his calls in Wimbledon.

Usually I would meet up with a select group of friends – all reps for well-known whisky or gin companies – at Fortnums' soda fountain at about ten in the morning. There we would discuss our day's programme and often arrange to meet up for lunch. Business in those days was conducted in a sociable and lighthearted way.

An agreeable part of my duties was to visit the leading West End hotels bars. The object was to become well acquainted with the head barmen to ensure that my brands were in a prominent position behind the bars and that the products were being used. My method was to tip liberally. On subsequent visits if the barman failed to recognize me or know my name I would double up the gratuity. I soon acquired the reputation of being a generous fellow and became well known in all the leading bars.

All these sort of calls entailed having a drink or two and more often than not I would run into friends in the trade which would call for a few more sharpeners. Usually a late lunch was the order of the day. Bentley's, the oyster restaurant, was one of my favourites. There I was well known to the staff and the hours were flexible. Very little work was done after lunch largely because I did not usually feel in a fit state. Besides, apart from afternoon drinking clubs, the bars shut at three pm. Often I would go back to Boodle's to sleep it off.

Two or three nights a week I had to get into my dinner jacket to attend a licensed victuallers banquet. These functions were considered by my boss to be a good opportunity to meet the trade, though I have to say that I came to find them tedious to a degree. One had to listen to boring speeches as well as eat and drink far too much. The affairs were more often than not held at the Connaught Rooms, off Kingsway, an uninspiring venue.

Wear and tear on dinner jackets was considerable; I had three which I used to wear in rotation. Often, together with a few friends, I would get the bit between my teeth and go on to a night club – usually a place with a good supply of attractive and available hostesses. The Embassy Club in Mayfair was a particular haunt of mine. On one occasion at this establishment, Jack, a colleague in the firm, became very drunk and aggressive. He had a row with the management and was escorted out by the 'heavies'. At the entrance he took a swipe at the doorman and knocked him out cold. Meanwhile I was having a splendid time below, surrounded by girls and drinks and quite oblivious as to what was going on upstairs. As it turned out, the management was quite unconcerned about the incident. After all I was spending money like water and they considered doormen to be expendable – and easily replaced.

In the early hours of the morning I received an anxious telephone call at Boodles', where I was staying, from Jack, recounting his unfortunate experience. He was very worried that we might have lost the account and that he himself might be fired. Nothing of the sort happened. Red Label continued to sell briskly and was made the pouring whisky at the Embassy. Provided you are a good spender in these sort of places, it seems, anything goes. Another time it was suggested by Arthur, the sales director, that I should take a party of American distributors to a night club after a lavish private dinner at the Hyde Park Hotel. Barry, their spokesman, was duly briefed and was told to take the party to the Embassy and that I would follow along later after I had fulfilled a previous appointment at Les Ambassadeurs.

Barry was assured that his party would be well received at the club and that they were to make themselves at home. I duly turned up and was horrified to find that all the Americans had not only procured girls for themselves but were dishing out presents in a most liberal fashion – big boxes of chocolates, nylons, cartons of cigarettes, not to mention champagne for the girls and bottles of whisky for themselves. My immediate concern was: 'Who's going to pay for all this?' I could see trouble looming and possibly the sack for letting the party get out of hand. I followed Barry down to the loo and casually said to him, whilst we were relieving ourselves in the stalls: 'Look Barry, your fellows seem to have gone berserk. There is going to be a big bill. Will you split it with me?'

'Not on your nelly, Hugo,' laughed Barry. 'You asked us here, you pay.'

In due time the account, amounting to six to seven hundred pounds, arrived at the office. Full of apprehension, I took it in to Arthur's room for signature before payment. After ticking me off for unnecessary expenditure he signed the bill and had the grace to admit that it was he who had suggested that I should take them on to a night club. At today's costs the bill would have been well into the thousands.

I met Barry, who was a decent enough chap, on quite a few subsequent occasions and it is reported that he is still laughing over the incident today. At least all the American distributors agreed that it was one of the best nights they had ever had in their lives. Very few of them went home to their hotel that night: they seemed particularly quiet and subdued at an export meeting the next day.

14

Wentworth

I have never been particularly good at golf although I played quite a lot during my sojourn in Scotland. Yet I enjoyed the game and always hoped to improve. Now, finding myself living at Wentworth, with the seventeenth fairway running alongside the garden, this was a great opportunity to do so.

The hierarchy at Walkers, with the Braid family and the DCL in general, slanted towards golf and it seemed to be important for my career to get to grips with the great old game. My target was the Cumming Trophy, for handicaps of twelve and above, played at Walton Heath in the DCL spring meeting. To achieve this, tuition and practice were necessary.

As the London rep I was not office-bound and indeed no-one knew where I was most of the time. I decided to go easy on the juice in the mornings and have lessons at the nets in Simpsons of Piccadilly during the afternoons. This tuition, together with evening practice at Wentworth, improved my game out of all recognition. Often I would go out on my own for nine holes playing against 'the Colonel' (Bogey), accompanied by Bruce, my dog. For someone who is not what they term a 'natural golfer' I was surprised at what improvement can be gained from practice and application. In the garden, too, I would practice wedge shots over the wired-in tennis court.

At the weekends I would usually have a game or two with friends who lived about. I got to know the courses at Wentworth well and my knowledge against a newcomer would be worth quite a few strokes. I had some agreeable games with Ernest Lisbourne, Gordon Goodhew, Don Griffin (Commander of the American 6th Fleet) and had a long-running battle with Chester Nimmitz, who was the most enthusiastic golfer I ever met. He would play in rain, sleet or snow and still enjoy it.

As a joke Liz Goodhew and I decided to enter for the Wentworth mixed foursomes – a knock-out competition. To our surprise we found ourselves in the final and went on to win it. Later we were very proud to see our names on the club house wall under the heading, The Pam Trophy.

All this was very useful training for the Cumming Trophy at Walton Heath, which I duly won. This achievement opened up new horizons: I was no longer an entire rabbit. I had joined the DCL golfing elite, albeit poor in comparison to some of them, but at least I had earned my spurs. Now I was invited to play midweek in various society competitions.

The garden at House in the Wood, as our new home was called, amounted to about four acres in all with a drive through a mature woodland of rhododendrons, oak, birch and chestnut trees, where badgers and foxes were not at all uncommon. The front garden, with an extensive lawn interspersed with rose beds, azaleas and other flowering shrubs, ran down to the seventeenth fairway of the Burma Road course. At the tip of the garden, which jutted out into the fairway, there were half a dozen good sized birch trees. These presented a hazard to ambitious golfers who tried to cut the corner. Consequently quite a number of golf balls ended up in the garden. Although the garden was out of bounds to the golfers, I permitted them to come through one of the gates to retrieve the ball if they could see it. On one occasion, to my horror, I spied from the house an errant golfer hacking at a ball in the rose bed. I charged out, hurling abuse at the bad mannered golfer who fled for his life.

On the whole the golfers behaved pretty well and respected private property. But once, when I was attending to some shrubs and roses on the edge of the golf course, I was hit in the back by a golf ball going at some speed. I was bending over at the time and the impact, which was quite painful, made me leap up. As chance would have it, I was alongside a rambling rose which scraped my eye. My immediate reaction was to rub the eye with my muddy hand: not the best thing to do. The eye got worse and became very painful, while the golf ball bruise was soon forgotten. I was carted off to hospital where it was established that my eyeball had received a nasty scratch from a rose thorn. For a week or so afterwards I went around with a large dressing over my eye which was secured by a bandage which practically covered my whole head.

Gardening near a golf course can be a dangerous occupation. To add insult to injury the golfer was unaware of the incident. After striking me the ball bounced back on to the fairway . . . .

IN the end I decided to gain my revenge by planting up a mass of heathers under the birch trees. I reaped a good harvest of golf balls. It was rather like collecting free range chicken's eggs: I would go out most evenings and usually find at least half a dozen balls.

My wife Dot was a good spender on the property. When she bought the place the house was a nice yellowy brown colour – not dissimilar to Cotswold stone. She immediately had it painted white, saying that she only liked living in white houses. She built a hard tennis court on the woodland side of the house, followed by a swimming pool alongside the house on the old vegetable plot. This suited me well enough because it reduced the gardening area; besides I enjoyed swimming. Unfortunately I was the only one in the family who knew how to change the water, clean the pool and work the filter. Many hours were spent on these tasks.

Dot also had the double garage converted into a play room for Caroline and William. Naturally *another* double garage had to be built on, not to mention the addition of a study with a dressing room above. Painters and decorators were continuously at work both inside and outside the house. Dot liked everything to look spick and span at all times.

On one memorable summer day I invited a number of my colleagues from Johnnie Walker, together with some of the advertising agency people, to a party round the pool. The booze was flowing freely and it was a wonder no-one was drowned. The last guest to leave slid into the back seat of his car and was puzzled as to why he was unable to drive away. I myself was no slouch when it came to enjoying a drink; indeed it was one of the pitfalls of my trade. After a busy day I would often come back home rather over the top and, having got the taste, would open the cupboard and pour myself another. Dot did not take kindly to this and on quite a few occasions she would go to the cupboard, extract all the Johnnie Walker bottles and pour them out of the study windows – what a waste! But at least the hydrangeas flourished. They were a most beautiful blue colour with lovely foliage.

The Wentworth and Sunningdale area, known as 'Rhododendria', has always been renowned for lavish parties. Fancy dress was popular, many of the outfits being hired from the London theatrical costumiers Nathans. On one such occasion Dot and I gave a lift to our next door neighbour Denise to a party in Sunningdale. She was a Swiss lady, very sexy and attractive. Denise was dressed up as a 'lady of easy virtue' and I went as a pirate. After supper, lots of champagne and dancing, I found a quiet unoccupied room where Denise and I got together for a spot of canoodling. But suddenly the door burst open and Dot came steaming in. She found us in a most intimate embrace. We were hustled off quickly into the car where on the way home Dot delivered herself of some nasty insults. Her parting shot to Denise was 'You came as a tart, you looked like a tart and you behaved like a tart'.

Caroline and William went to little schools at Virginia Water and Sunninghill respectively. Afterwards Caroline went on to Heathfield and William to Heatherdown and Eton. Their education was worked out geographically: they were never far from each other or from home, thereby cutting down time and expense for *exeats*, half terms and so forth.

It was, on the whole, a happy time with plenty of laughs, though on the work front there was the odd spot of friction inevitable in a large business. Stuck in my position as London representative I was having a certain amount of trouble with Arthur, my sales director; though possibly this statement should be phrased the other way round. At any rate I was narked about a few minor instructions being imposed upon me, so I decided to have a bit of fun with Arthur and the old firm.

One day walking around Soho in the course of my travelling duties, I came across some buskers known as the Happy Wanderers. I had an idea. I approached the group and asked if they would come to St James's Street and play their hearts out outside No 63, Walker's head office. The spokesman was a bit reluctant to start with, saying that it was illegal for street musicians to play in 'that toff part of the West End' in the middle of clubland. But with the aid of a few green notes they agreed to strike up the band that afternoon;. I then stationed myself at my club, Boodles, across the road in order to avail myself of a good view. The Happy Wanderers duly arrived and started playing, much to the amusement of passers by. The reaction at Walker's head office was tremendous. The staff to a man downed tools, opened the windows and cheered, showering the musicians with coins.

After a few minutes, with the buskers playing *Colonel Bogey* for all their worth, I observed a furious Arthur leaning out of his window and shouting at them to go away. Indeed it was not long before they were obliged to do so. They had spied a copper on his way down from Piccadilly so they scarpered.

15

Bart on Board

I was holding my father's hand when he died in bed at his home. We had always been close to each other and indeed we looked very much alike. Father had been a regular soldier in the Royals, seeing service in the Boer War and the Great War, before settling in Shropshire to look after the family estate. He was a proper traditional squire, enjoying the usual country pursuits such as hunting, shooting and fishing; indeed he was Master of the local pack of foxhounds. He also did his fair share of public work as a magistrate and county councillor.

His two eldest sons had been killed in the Second World War, which was a shattering blow and one from which he never really recovered. For my part, now the eldest surviving son, I felt I now belonged to the life of commerce. I had entered this way of life at eighteen and felt I was best suited to continue to carry on in the same way.

The local wheelwright, Harry Jones, had a side-line making coffins in our little village of Bedstone and he produced a superb one for my father, his landlord. Harry was also the local undertaker and prepared my father's body for the coffin. Half a dozen tenants in their best suits appeared at the house to carry down the coffin which was placed on a bier before being pushed up quite a steep hill to rest overnight at the village church in readiness for the funeral the next day.

Harry led the sombre procession and all went well until they got about halfway up the hill. Then he stopped and came back to have a word with me in the rear of the pushing party. Meanwhile the bier was gently freewheeling down the hill again until one of the tenants found a large stone and stuck it under the wheel. Harry, a little agitated, wanted to know if I had got the death certificate because the funeral could not take place without it, and it was irregular to place the body in church without one.

No one had thought about a death certificate and as it was the weekend it seemed likely to be difficult to find a registrar to sign one. The bier was pushed on up to the churchyard and I set off in my car to look for the official. I arrived in Clun, the nearest place, but the man was away. After a good deal of misdirection, I eventually succeeded in finding a registrar in Bishops Castle, who did the necessary. Harry was very relieved when I returned to the church brandishing the document about two hours later.

The funeral took place the next day, with all the family present. The coffin was lowered into the family vault by the tenants.

On my return to work in London everyone seemed most surprised that I now had a title. I had never divulged that my father was a Baronet and that I was in line to succeed. The board's reaction was one of puzzlement. They had never encountered this situation before. While they were all perfectly satisfied with my work and felt that I would, in due time, go on to the higher eschelons, I was still only forty years old – which in those days was considered to be far too young for a seat on the board. It was very rare for an employee to become a director until he was in his fifties and had at least twenty years service. I had only been with the firm for nine years.

Arthur's immediate reaction – he was always very commercially minded – was to suggest that I should expand my calls to the larger customers who might be impressed by 'my handle'. Useful contacts would be made, Arthur felt, which in the long run would result in extra business. I was not agreeable to this idea and refused to use my title in any commercial sense whatsoever.

Although I was keen to continue in my business career I realized that I would need to spend a certain amount of time looking after the family properties in Bradford and Shropshire. And so, after a great deal of thought, I decided to issue an ultimatum to the firm. Either I would be put on the board immediately or I would leave. At least, I felt, I would find out what the directors thought of me and whether or not I was considered to be indispensable or expendable. After a week's suspense I was called into the managing director's office and invited to join the board. It transpired later that Arthur had put in a good word for me and that probably swung the issue. Together with George, the production director at Kilmarnock, I was duly elected at the next board meeting.

The following Monday, now a director, I decided to behave like one and arrived at the office at ten am. Unfortunately I had been expected earlier than this for some minor meeting – not previously announced – and was asked by Harry, the managing director, why I was late. I made some crazy comment to the effect that now I was a director and could suit myself about office hours. Harry was not best pleased and told me in no uncertain manner that directors of the company arrived before the staff and usually stayed later. As the years went by I came to consider this dictum to be complete tripe. Indeed I was to have the last laugh, as the story will unfold.

About this time a comic incident occurred in the lift. A young trainee, Colin, arrived in the office late – about ten thirty am. He had the misfortune to enter the lift on the ground floor at the same time as Harry. Thinking quickly, Colin remarked to Harry: 'A bit foggy down your way too, Sir?' In fact it was a beautiful day and Harry had merely been visiting one of the departments downstairs, having arrived as usual at eight am. Harry, who had a good sense of humour, often recounted this incident with a chuckle.

For my pains, I was appointed a junior home sales director under Arthur. Besides the usual office routine – Arthur used to off-load a lot of boring stuff on to me – every letter had to be answered the same day. Most of them, I may say, were of an extremely trivial nature.

I was always encouraged to get out and make calls every day. In the London area, which was taken over by Euan Johnston, a young ex-Grenadier of great charm and enthusiasm who has remained a good friend to this day, I would visit wholesalers, West End hotels and clubs – sometimes with Euan and sometimes on my own. On top of this, Arthur decided that I should take over responsibility for the north of England and keep contact with the rep up there. This suited me well as I was able to combine business trips with visits to the family mill property in Bradford.

I liked the north and had happy memories of an earlier visit to Harrogate with Arthur's peppery predecessor, Smithy. We were touring round the West Riding of Yorkshire with Duncan, the man in charge of the north. Smithy, as you will recall, had a great liking and a remarkable capacity for Red Label. Consequently he was not very fit. Yet he was always immaculately dressed and had a great presence. As we returned in a heavy snow storm from Leeds, the car, driven by Duncan, stuck on the steep hill just outside Harrogate. Smithy and I got out and started to push the vehicle. After we had expended a great deal of energy, the tread of the tyres at last got a grip, but in the course of our exertions we were covered by showers of snow and grit. Duncan kept going and proceeded up the hill for another half mile to make absolutely sure of level ground. Smithy and I slithered up the hill, my out of condition colleague effing and blinding with every step.

When we eventually reached the car, Smithy was in bad shape and extremely irate. He cursed Duncan and called him every name in the book, demanding to know why the devil he had not stopped sooner. In fact Duncan had an old score to settle with Smithy, who was always something of a bully to his employees. Duncan had got his own back with a vengeance. He and I had a very good laugh about this incident.

16

Down Under

One afternoon in the autumn of 1956, for some reason or another, I was digging a deep pit in the woodland area of our house at Wentworth. My wife Dot came along and said: 'Surely that's deep enough – you will be hitting Australia soon.' By a curious coincidence, the very next day I was summoned to the managing director's office at Walker's and told that I had been selected to go on a six week tour of Australia and New Zealand on behalf of the firm in a week's time.

The Antipodean market had traditionally been visited by the managing director only, and in fact no-one from Britain had been out there since pre-war days. Harry, the managing director, explained that on medical advice it would be unwise for him to make the trip and that he felt I would be a good substitute to take his place. Indeed Harry did not like travelling and rarely went abroad; if he did so he almost invariably fell sick and returned early. All arrangements had been made for my Down Under adventure and the best accommodation had been fixed up.

I returned home that evening and told Dot that she must have had a premonition about Australia. She went quite white and could not believe it. She then imagined all sorts of dangers and problems and was particularly angry about there being no question – as there wasn't in those days – of a wife accompanying her husband on such a journey.

The next week in the office was spent familiarizing myself with the state of the markets in the various Australian states and in New Zealand. I checked all my schedules and enjoyed buying, at the firm's expense, suitable luggage and tropical clothing. It was reminiscent of my setting off for Ceylon some twenty years earlier. This time, however, I was travelling not by boat but by aeroplane. I embarked on a Constellation from Heathrow, travelling first class and in great comfort. This huge, and rather slow, aeroplane was to become my home for the next few days. We stopped off to refuel at Rome, Bahrain, Calcutta and Singapore before finally landing at Perth in Western Australia. There were regular changes of crew along the line.

Bahrain was probably the hottest place I have ever encountered. The airport consisted of a series of lean-to huts and the heat was unbearable. Piedogs were lying around in what shade there was, panting with their tongues out. I decided on a short walk to the perimeter fence where I met up with a Cameronian soldier on duty. 'How do you like it out here?' I asked him.

'Bloody awful – it's too fucking hot,' the soldier replied.

'Surely it's not as bad as all that; you can slip into the sea over there and have a swim when you feel like it.'

'You can't do that, the water is full of sea serpents.'

If that was true it would certainly have deterred me.

Calcutta airport was quite up to date and bliss compared to Bahrain. It was full of well-to-do Indians who presumably used it regularly to obtain alcoholic refreshment since it was difficult to get whisky in India at that time. The flight at night across the Bay of Bengal was very bumpy indeed and it was one of the few times that I really was thankful to be strapped into a seat belt. For some reason the trip over this bit of ocean is often scary and uncomfortable.

At Singapore I was met by Johnnie Walker's agent who was a part-time ADC to the Governor. A huge young fellow, about six feet seven inches tall, he was well connected and had the reputation of being a bit of a lad. Evidently having 'fixed' the airport officials and customs people had had stationed himself close to the disembarking area. As the passengers came off he was looking out for his 'Sir' whom he had imagined to be an elderly and intimidating old buffer. After a few false introductions he was highly surprised to meet a fairly youngish, easy going sort of chap who himself had the reputation of being a bit of a lad.

On recovering from the shock, the agent took control of the situation. Calling on his VIP/ADC experience, he whisked me through customs and other formalities to a chauffeur-driven car and we headed straight for the legendary Raffles Hotel.

I was delighted to be staying in this splendid old hotel. I was fascinated by the building itself and revelled in the old world courtesy. Mysterious pretty Chinese girls glided gracefully around the shop area of the hotel but, as a newcomer, I was uncertain whether or not they were 'on the game'. I subsequently learnt that a word to 'the boy' could produce an attractive female in my room with no trouble at all. Yet I had little time for activities of this sort. I was kept busy morning, noon and night during my brief stop over in Singapore in the interests of the old firm. There were visits to be made to wholesalers, hotels and shops besides luncheons and dinner parties.

One such dinner party we held at the restaurant of a smart new hotel and the guests included the colonels of the British regiments stationed in Singapore together with two or three beautiful and well-connected Chinese girls. Looks from the other tables registered surprise and disapproval. Besides being stunning girls who talked perfect English they had panache and humour. Seated between two of them I had one of the best evenings of my whole trip.

My first visit to Chinatown, where a great deal of liqueur is sold, was a source of amazement. I felt as if there was a festival going on or even that the flags had been put out especially for me. But it was merely Chinese washing hanging out on sticks to dry. Throngs of people virtually blocked the thoroughfares. Every other shop displayed crispy roast duckling, with live ducks and chickens in cages alongside. All accounting and calculation were done accurately by beads on a form of grille. Sometimes I would bump into a large dead snake hanging down from a post or the awning of a shop. Python is considered quite a delicacy, I believe.

Walking down a busy street one morning in Singapore, I was greatly amused when a very pretty young Chinese girl greeted the agent with much affection. To her amazement he walked straight on – clearly she was one of his mistresses. I also noticed a more modest look of recognition from other girls. The agent turned out to be a well known philanderer with the locals.

For the afternoons I was handed over to the Chinese rep to call on various Chinese establishments. He was a charming little fellow, quite old, but with a good sense of fun. His command of English, however, was not too good. In order to get an idea of the drinking habits of the local population I asked about the relative popularity of the three main spirits -that is to say brandy, whisky and gin. The Chinese rep replied: 'Brandy most popular. Chinese people like girls very much. Very good for *that*!'

He then gave a graphic demonstration of what he meant by closing his fist and moving his arm up to his elbow in a very vigorous fashion, accompanied by a huge grin. He continued, 'Whisky quite good', and demonstrated this by the arm movement in a less vigorous manner. 'But *red* Chinese lucky colour. So Johnnie Walker Red Label best whisky.'

I reminded him about the gin. He said: 'Gin no good – makes knees tremble.'

Geoffrey and I became good friends and drinking companions during the short stay. In fact he did a good job for the brand, albeit in an unconventional way. Alas, he was fired soon afterwards for various misdemeanours, but perhaps this was not altogether surprising.

The next stop on my journey to Australia, Jakarta, was uncomfortable and rather scary. Evidently there had been some internal turmoil in the country. On landing, the plane was immediately surrounded by soldiers with tommy guns, and the passengers were rudely escorted by another posse of soldiers with automatic guns to the airport buildings. We were herded into a small hot room – no air-conditioning – and left there for some hours. Eventually all of us in turn were obliged to go up to a desk and declare what money we had on us and show it. At long last passports were stamped. I never discovered what the reason for all this performance was. Certainly it delayed the flight which was due to arrive in Perth, Western Australia at about six am the next morning.

Bert, the Australian general manager had flown from Sydney, about two thousand miles away, to meet me at the airport. We were already quite good friends, having worked together at the office in London, but he was not best pleased at his early start and having to hang around for four or five hours. Perhaps he was trying to get his own back when he announced that we were to go off immediately to the mayor's parlour to meet the Lord Mayor.

The first encounter with anyone in a different country, let

alone the chief citizen of the state, tends to bring out a degree of apprehension and shyness. This situation prevailed during the first twenty minutes of my meeting with Lord Mayor in his parlour notwithstanding gallant attempts by Bert to ease things along. But then, unexpectedly, the Lord Mayor announced: 'I think we should have a drink.' A bottle of Red Label was duly produced and a good measure was poured out in the glasses of everyone present. The change in atmosphere was quite remarkable. Good animated conversation flowed. The Lord Mayor turned out to be a thoroughly good bloke – a useful imbiber with a fine sense of humour. I was to meet him two or three times afterwards during my stay in Western Australia.

I found Perth, on the Swan River, to be a beautiful place. It is reported to be the most remote city in the world judged by its distance from any other city. Over breakfast the next morning at the old hotel where Bert and I were putting up, I was struck by the way our fellow guests addressed themselves to the pleasures of the table. There was no conversation whatever. Heads were down and all one heard was a clatter of knives and forks hitting the plates. Most of them were eating large steaks.

Besides the usual business rounds, receptions and so forth, I was given a tour of the area. Among other more attractive places, I was shown the red light district. It reminded me of nothing so much as a series of cages in which the late Guy the Gorilla was housed in London Zoo. The girls had their wired-in compounds where they displayed themselves, with shanties or shacks behind in which they got down to business. No doubt just the stuff for sex-starved drovers, prospectors and outback men. This was a perfectly legalized operation. It was found to be beneficial to the police in apprehending suspects and criminals in this controlled grey area. Furthermore, it kept the girls off the streets.

Inter-state air travel in Australia was highly efficient. Like advertisements on television for British Midland the passenger arrives a few minutes before the plane sets off, similar to catching a London bus, and travels in comfort to his destination. We proceeded without mishap to Adelaide – probably best known for the cricketer Don Bradman and the Barossa Valley, the wine growing area. We met Fred, the South Australian distributor, who gave me a useful tip. Seeing that I was a 'newie' and perhaps a bit of a 'toff' he suggested that I didn't want to worry about the Sir bit: 'We don't care about that sort of thing out here. Instead of being introduced with all that paraphernalia, get into the place wherever you are, put out your hand and say: 'I am Hugo'. That was good advice and I stuck to it throughout my tour.

The South Australian Hotel was a splendid old colonial type of place with surprisingly good food. A fellow called Carl was the restaurant, food and beverage concessionaire – all in one – rather an unusual arrangement. He was probably Swiss, but could have been Austrian. Carl had been there for many years and was well known throughout Australia in the hotel world, partly because of his culinary expertise and partly because of his wealth. For his holidays he usually flew to Sydney and took a suite at the five star Australia Hotel. I soon learnt that Australians, like Americans, respect success and money.

As luck would have it, a troupe of cabaret girls happened to be staying at the hotel whilst we were there. Needless to say, I moved in fast – to the embarrassment of Bert, who was trying to portray his director as a senior and important person. My recollection of my first night at the hotel was hazy, to say the least. Whether or not I 'made it', I never discovered. Certainly I woke up with a severe head the next morning. The hour or two spent at Fred's office after breakfast turned out to be an important discussion on South Australian trade affairs. I am afraid my contribution was non-existent. I was relieved when it was suggested we should make a few calls on licensed establishments in the city.

It seemed that everyone knew Fred in this pleasantly under-crowded capital city of a fairly backward state. Starting with the Three Musketeers the 'followers' increased at each pub (known as an 'hotel' in Australia) we visited. By the time we reached the third boozer there was a gang of twenty or more in our wake. They were not scroungers, they merely liked a good booze-up. There would be a mad rush to the bar to register their 'shout' to the licensee.

At each call – and there were seven or eight that morning – everyone present had to have his 'shout'. Not one person moved off without doing his round.

It was heavy drinking, but not so bad as might be imagined. Bottles of Johnnie Walker Red Label were placed on the bar and everyone helped themselves, the licensee taking a good account of each round. It did not take me too long to get wise to the situation. By placing my hand over the neck of the bottle I could, undetected, give myself a 'nobble' (a small one); but the licensee did very well indeed by charging the full price for every nip.

Having watched a game of Australian Rules football in Adelaide, and spent an agreeable day with the Gillespie family on their wine-growing estate in the Barossa Valley, Bert and I caught the plane for Melbourne. Frank Herman, the JW distributor in Victoria was a most charming man. Besides having built up a marvellous business for the firm he was well connected in the state. The two of us spent some of our time at a fine hotel in the city owned by Frank and the rest of the time at his country home on the Yarra river near Colstream.

On the station Frank had a fine pedigree herd of polled Herefords, which interested me because I had just started a similar venture on my property in Shropshire. It was strange to be woken up in the early hours of the morning by the raucous shrieks of a kookaburra bird (known as 'the laughing jackass'), which would be hunting around in the garden for snakes.

A big party was laid on in my honour at my hotel in Melbourne – the first of many during my tour of Australia. These affairs all took a similar sort of form: lots to eat and drink until about halfway through when the host would call for silence and announce that I would like to say a few words. This was unexpected and distinctly off-putting on the first occasion. But all went well and at least I now knew what to expect at future parties.

Frank had assembled a grand crowd of people including the Premier and some ministers. Bolte, the Premier, a regular Black Label man, became a good friend and later I was able to play a return match by taking him out to lunch at the Ritz in London when he was over for the Commonwealth Games.

Bert and I spent quite a lot of time at the Melbourne Club, similar in every way – leather armchairs and all – to London's clubland. It seemed that practically all the members, including ministers, had sheep and cattle stations in the outback.

A day at the races was one of the highlights of our stay in Melbourne. Many English racecourses could take a leaf out of their book for comfort, viewing and entertaining facilities.

Indeed I thought Melbourne a gracious city, very different to our next port of call.

I found Sydney a bustling city with new buildings and skyscrapers much on the American lines. I was particularly struck by the homes of the rich alongside the 'bridge' and stretching down into the estuary. They were quite small but very comfortable with usually a few acres of ground and, of course, all the latest mod cons and gadgets. The prices were staggering, mostly in the region of half-a-million pounds and above. Practically all the other old homesteads had been pulled down. It was noticeable that the Sydney people had little respect for anything old. There were some splendid beaches around the city and the locals made full use of them. Bondi Beach was a seething mass of bronzed humanity most of the year round with teams of professional life savers, together with shark spotters. It was very rare for a shark to go undetected.

At Bondi and certain other beaches in the area there was what the locals call a 'rip'. This is a deeper channel which is encountered soon after the bather has paddled into the sea. It is about waist to shoulder height and afterwards it becomes quite shallow again until the swimmer gets out into the ocean proper. Over the years many people have been taken by sharks in the rip, which is surprisingly close to the shore. Most of the private properties and private beaches in the estuary harbour area, where there were always sharks – probably attracted by blood from abattoirs – had shark-proof safety barriers, composed of permanent uprights with steel-linked chain fencing.

I met the opera singer Joan Hammond's brother, who had a few hotels in Sydney and who also acted as a part-time life saver. He told me of a nasty experience he once had. He was coming in on a surf board at Bondi in quite a big sea when he noticed a large man-eating shark swimming alongside him. The brute kept with him through the rip and right to the shore. Fortunately, being an expert surfer, he kept his head and did not fall off.

Although a very junior director of the firm, I was representing the managing director and so was given the most enormous suite in the Australian Hotel in Sydney. I did a certain amount of entertaining there, but I found it particularly useful as a place to exercise, thereby getting rid of the excess liquor I had consumed during the day. Walkers had a friendly little office in Sydney which was Bert's headquarters. Throughout the state of New South Wales they had their own selling organization with reps and so forth. The business in all the other states was conducted by distributors, under the direction of Bert. The office had a reputation of being a good port of call for visitors. Invariably before lunch, and again for an evening session, people would call in and receive the usual hospitality.

This was by no means confined to the trade. Judges, ministers, bankers and all sorts would drop in. That was one of the big differences I noticed between commercial life in Australia and Britain. Down under, the top people had no airs or graces and everyone settled into Christian-name terms straight away.

Next Bert and I found ourselves *en route* for Brisbane, the capital of Queensland. The flight was rather unusual and a bit scary. Below in the scrub there were a whole series of forest fires. Then we were caught up in the middle of a big electric storm. At the time I was reading a story about an early flight from Sydney to Brisbane which disappeared mysteriously in the bush when suddenly there was a tremendous bang with flashes of lightning everywhere with the plane dropping like a lead weight. We learned later that the aircraft had been struck by lightning; fortunately the conductor worked as it was supposed to.

Flying over Brisbane was a wonderfully colourful experience. The plane made a circle of the city in brilliant sunshine. Looking out of the window I was amazed to see an almost complete canopy of brilliant bluey-mauve. I was lucky to see the Jacaranda trees in full blossom. They thrive particularly well up there and there are masses of them. The illusion from the air was easy to understand because the branches of the trees spread out over a wide area in the form of gigantic table tops.

The two of us lunched at Lennon's Hotel where another surprise awaited me: all the ladies wore big decorative hats and smart clothes. It was no special occasion, but it looked as if they were all off to the Royal Meeting at Ascot.

Having done a bit of work in the city, Bert, knowing my interest in agriculture and the outback, fixed up a trip with some contacts further inland. We set off with a driver to the

Darwin Downs which I expected to be some sort of prairie at sea level. It was nothing of the sort. We climbed and climbed for some thousands of feet along a minor road which eventually turned into a dirt road. A remarkable vista, away from the gum trees, opened up. A plateau stretching as far as the eye could see presented itself. It was as flat as a pancake, with miles and miles of beautiful corn crops, mostly wheat with some maize and barley.

Bert and I were well received by the owners of the station and we sat out on the verandah of this large colonial-type of bungalow enjoying a glass of cool beer. I detected a Jeep, throwing up clouds of dust, approaching from the far distance. As it got closer I was puzzled because there did not seem to be a driver at the wheel. Eventually the Jeep arrived at good speed at the bungalow and I was astonished to see a very small person leap out from the driving seat. It was the farmer's daughter, aged ten or under, returning to lunch from school. On making enquiries, I was told that she always drove herself to school and back – and had been doing so ever since her feet could touch the pedals.

After a good lunch we took a walk around the prairie. There had been no rain for a long time and there were enormous cracks in the soil, yet the crops were magnificent. I asked the farmer if he had to put in a lot of fertilizer. He replied that he never put in any, adding that it was quite unnecessary. Evidently the Darwin Downs were one of the most fertile areas in the whole of Australia and the top soil goes down to a depth of ten feet or more.

Twice during the our walk we came across tiger snakes, which slithered off into the corn. They are deadly poisonous and generally keep out of the way of human beings, yet caution should be exercised when going through and picking green crops. This encounter reminded me of an incident in, of all places, London. An Australian nurse working there telephoned to say that she had a snake in a Johnnie Walker bottle which she thought might be of interest to us. She duly turned up with the bottle and sure enough there was a long snake in perfect condition curled up in the sealed bottle of whisky.

Apparently as a child in Australia she was about to get into bed when to her horror she saw this tiger snake curled up in the bed. She alerted the family and her father came in and killed the snake. Probably because she had had such a lucky escape her father decided to pickle it in a bottle of Johnnie Walker Red Label. By way of a thank you for this remarkable object the young nurse received some bottles of Johnnie Walker. To this day the bottle with the snake in it remains in the firm's museum and creates a lot of interest.

From Brisbane we went to spend a few nights at Surfers Paradise, a popular holiday place for people all over Australia. One day we decided to go off with our distributor, a brewer, to a small house he owned a few miles south. It was an isolated house on the seashore with mile upon mile of silver sand in front of us with not a soul in sight. While we were changing preparatory to a swim I noticed spouts of water coming out of the sea. I was told it was a whale or, more probably, a school of whales. I found this rather disturbing, feeling that if there were whales around there would probably be sharks as well. I was told that it was the wrong time of the year for sharks to come in close along the coastline.

So the three of us set off across the empty, whispering sand. The whales seemed to have come in closer and they could now be seen quite clearly when they surfaced. I did not go very far out during that swim and made sure my two companions were well in front of me in case there happened to be a shark lurking about.

On the way back from Brisbane to Sydney I was keen to get my reports done so that I could have an afternoon's swim at Bondi. I set up my little dictaphone and yacked on about trade in Queensland. It never occurred to me that the noise in the aircraft – quite an ancient one – would practically obliterate every word. This was my usual method of relaying information back to London. On my return to head office I asked my secretary whether the tapes had been all right. She replied that if she disregarded the 'ums' and 'ahs', not to mention the many fruity expletives, she got the general gist of the thing. But on the Queensland report there had seemed to be a terrible buzzing noise in the background, and she could not make head or tail of the thing. Nonetheless the report was duly typed out and made good reading – including the bit about Queensland. I asked: 'How the hell did you fix that one?'

She replied: 'We have got our resources here and there *is* such a thing as a *telephone*'.

I spent a few more days in Sydney. One agreeable excursion was a trip down the harbour in a police launch accompanied by the chief. He had a good supply of refreshment aboard.

The Sydney hoteliers and licensees decided to throw a party followed by luncheon at which I was the guest of honour. This was a very liquid affair and after lunch, in singularly good form by now, I staggered to my feet and made what I thought was an excellent off-the-cuff speech. On sitting down, I turned to Bert and said: 'Was that all right?'

To my consternation Bert replied: 'It was bloody awful, you went on far too long. You didn't give the others long enough to speak. Surely you must have learnt by now that Aussies love to get up and spout. You *hogged* it and they don't like that.'

It was probably just as well that we were off to Tasmania the next day. We booked in at the main hotel in Launceston, a very old fashioned place where all bars in the town shut at six pm. This followed the 'five to six swill' when the local population seemed bent on throwing as much booze down their throats as they possibly could in a short space of time. After six pm the streets were deserted. There was not a soul in sight.

Food was plentiful at the hotel; plates were piled high and untrimmed steaks would flop over the side of the plate. Bert and I were having lunch there one day and asked the waitress, a tiny, thin slip of a girl, what she recommended. After a bit of chat, she said she thought we should go for a steak – adding that she had had one for breakfast and that it was in prime condition.

Bert and I set off in a self-drive car from Launceston to Hobart. It was a beautiful trip, with the countryside in parts rather reminiscent of the Welsh border country. Flowering broom and gorse along the roadside made a pretty picture. About halfway to our destination we called in to see a new friend, whom I had met in the plane coming out. It transpired that he was a well-known personality in Tasmania with a lovely house set in the middle of a huge station. We went round the place in a Land Rover, inspecting large flocks of merino sheep and a grand herd of pedigree polled Herefords. The estate was beautifully maintained, with miles of New Zealand-type wire fencing separating the lush fields with the bush, which was composed of scrub and gum trees.

Back at the house, Bert and I were entertained in a highly

civilized fashion. Although we handed over our bottles of Johnnie Walker our host was insistent that we should all fill our cups with an aged and special brew of whisky which he dispensed from a large earthenware vessel. It was strong, but fine stuff. Bert and I continued our journey south in a very merry state but reached Hobart without incident.

Hobart is particularly renowned for three things: its brewing, which was the reason for our visit; a fine harbour, with anchorage for large ships (the *Queen Mary* pulled in there a number of times during the Second World War) and Mount Cook, which dominates the town. In earlier years, at the time of a depression and unemployment, the state decided to build a road to the top of the mountain. It was quite an engineering feat; quite useless, of course, but of great scenic value and at least it kept the people in work. Perhaps a lesson could be learnt here for the unemployment situation in Britain.

Bert and I had a great trip up the mountain, encountering many hairpin bends until we reached the top which, to our surprise, was covered in snow. I am sorry to say we indulged in a snowball match rather than enjoy what must have been a remarkable view of Hobart, the ocean and the countryside around. Mount Cook is virtually a forest and the old eucalyptus trees which grow there are probably the finest specimens in the world.

At the time of our visit to Hobart there was a fair amount of excitement over Sputnik I; the city was supposed to be a prime viewing place. Most of the population went outside, including Bert and myself, at the allocated time. It was certainly seen by many people, but the two visitors, having been entertained very well beforehand, were not at all certain that they had seen the object although it was a beautifully clear evening with the stars shining brightly.

Tasmania was the final Australian state on my itinerary. In fact, my trip had included all the states with the exception of the Northern Territory. Bert and I motored back to Launceston and took a plane on to Sydney. This was the parting of the ways – indeed sadly I have never seen Bert from that day to this.

* * *

I set off on the next leg of my Antipodean travels, this time by Teal airways to New Zealand. I was met at Christchurch airport by Harry Nicholls of Quill Morris, the distributors. Harry was a delightful man; he had one or two heart attacks but never spared himself – whether it was work, sport or parties.

Soon after my arrival a big party was arranged to which a good cross-section of Christchurch had been invited. I remember this occasion particularly well for two reasons: first, because at the conclusion of my short speech a professor came up to me and introduced himself saying he was so pleased and interested to listen to me. It reminded him, the Prof said, of his young days in the Home Counties of England. Nobody in New Zealand talked like that and it was a great treat for him. He never referred to the content of the speech. The second reason was that I met Admiral Duffeck of the United States Navy. The Admiral had quite a few Globemaster aircraft on the runway at Christchurch which were used to ferry personnel, stores, food and equipment to their base on the South Pole. The Admiral kindly suggested that I should take a trip there with him next day. He felt he could make arrangements to fly the Johnnie Walker flat on a new territory.

Regretfully, I felt I should decline. My chairman in London might have taken a dim view if I had got stuck out there. At any rate, I was working to a tight schedule with flights and hotel accommodation booked up in advance.

My arrival in Christchurch coincided with a Labour Day holiday. Unbeknown to me, Harry had fixed up a trip into the interior with another sporting friend. We all set off in four-wheel drive vehicles containing bedding, cooking equipment, food and drink and eventually fetched up at a shepherd's hut in rugged and remote country near the Hurunui River. The idea was to go after the deer with a rifle. Unfortunately conditions were not quite right. The beasts were above the snow line and it would be impossible to get near them. Instead Bill, the other bloke, and I decided to go for a trek along the foothills in the hope of putting up a wild pig. We were walking through an area of long tufty grass when to our great surprise two pigs appeared quite close by in front of us. The pigs looked at the two of us, grunted and galloped off at a cracking pace.

My reaction was too slow. I might have got off a shot while

they were stationary. As it was I emptied a magazine at the rear pig, which was jumping around and travelling at a good speed, but I failed to register. After quite a long run our quarry found sanctuary in some thick and impenetrable thorn scrub, known locally as *matagari*. On reflection, it was probably as well the pigs withdrew. There could have been trouble had they charged. Our total bag was one goose shot on the banks of the river on the way back to the hut.

Meanwhile Harry had been busy preparing a good hot dinner for the party. The river was reported to be pretty good for rainbow trout. Unfortunately there was another week or two to go before the season opened.

On return to Christchurch, Harry threw a party at his home. A niece and nephew had been dispatched to the estuary of a nearby river to collect whitebait. At certain times of the year they are very plentiful and the children merely waded into the water with shrimping nets and returned with a good catch. I was instructed to cook the little fish in readiness for the party. On displaying ignorance about cooking whitebait, I was given a brief lesson by Harry and told to get on with it. The result was whitebait in batter – and very tasty it was too.

I was most impressed by the sheep and cattle stations in the South Island with their sumptuous pastures and most efficient fencing. The climate is so perfect that there is no need to winter stock in buildings as in England.

My next stop was at Dunedin, a quiet little place with a very strong Scottish contingent. It was snowing on my arrival and it was still snowing when I left. It was here that my itinerary was knocked on the head; indeed, it came to a full stop. I was supposed to go on to Invercargill, right down at the tip of New Zealand, then to the North Island, stopping at Wellington and Auckland. Then, by way of a change, I was routed back via Nandi in Fiji, Honolulu and San Francisco, but sadly this was not to be.

I had received a message that I was to return to Christchurch immediately. There I was told that my wife Dot was ill, having had some sort of breakdown. Apparently she was suffering from severe anxiety as a result of my trip and was down to about six and a half stone. There seemed to be no alternative but to fly home. I telephoned the firm in London and told them of my decision.

17

Licensed Victualler

A short time after my return home Dot and I, with Bruce the Labrador, went for a walk along one of the Wentworth estate roads. On the way home I 'came over all queer', and had to sit down on a tree stump. I had great difficulty in breathing. I was taken back by car and a doctor was summoned. There was no doubt the doctor was concerned because the breathing problem had by now become quite acute. He immediately telephoned Dr Bockner, the heart specialist in London, who promised to be with us in about an hour and a half's time.

On his arrival Dr Bockner set up his box of tricks, in fact a cardiograph. It turned out that I was suffering from severe exhaustion as a result of worry, fatigue, jet lag and so forth – there was nothing wrong with my heart. After a week confined to bed, I was restored to good health again.

It seemed at that time that my main occupation was the presidency of the Licensed Victuallers. I received a lot of publicity in the trade press and my old mug appeared in the *Morning Advertiser* regularly. One of the earliest banquets at which I presided was at Grantham. I was still quite new to the job and nervous and apprehensive about speaking in public. My practice was to write out my own speeches and then commit them to memory. This can be dangerous if you get stuck and find it necessary to refer to the text. It is embarrassing for all concerned when the speaker pauses over long, whilst frantically going through his notes in order to find out where he had got to.

On this particular occasion at Grantham, the victuallers were warmed up by a man playing good rousing Scottish airs with great gusto on a harmonium. The president, the chairman, the mayor and other dignitaries together with their ladies were gathered together in a private room for drinks before the banquet. The toastmaster – John Mills (not the diminutive thespian knight), whom I used to take around with me, announced that the procession was about to enter the main hall. Then the harmonium player went into a brisk march to which the procession was supposed to keep step to the accompaniment of loud hand claps. The geography of the place was such that the procession had to descend a long, narrow and steep stairway before entering the hall. It was at this stage in the proceedings that the Lady Mayoress, evidently trying to keep time with the harmonium, lost her footing and took a toss. She ended up at the foot of the stairway in a very undignified manner.

The local worthy was helped to her feet by all and sundry and proceeded to march off to her allotted place next to the president. I thought I detected a bit of a smile and a wink once we got to the table and I was relieved that the Lady Mayoress was not upset by the incident; at the same time I was a little concerned that she might have over-trained at the bar beforehand. My worst fears were confirmed within the next few minutes. The soup arrived safely at the top table. This is sometimes an anxious moment at a function of this sort and I had been the recipient of spillage on a number of occasions. When everything seemed to be going nicely, there was suddenly a tremendous clatter. The soup and the bowl disappeared from the table and landed on the Lady Mayoress's lap before crashing on to the floor.

The Lady Mayoress was in a terrible mess; but she did not seem unduly put out. Her only concern was that her handbag had gone down with the rest of the stuff. She went after it and I gallantly thought I had better do the same. So we both disappeared under the table. At the sprig adjoining the top table various Johnnie Walker people and guests were seated – including Gordon Melville, who was in charge of the firm's Birmingham office. Gordon was horrified by the turn of events and was convinced that the president (myself) had passed out under the table and that he (Gordon) would have to make the main speech of the evening. But the Lady Mayoress was duly wiped down and the evening ended up in the usual happy and alcoholic state.

Many banquets followed all over the country. After

Grantham, I went on to perform at Leicester. This was a big one at the Grand Hotel. In those days the firm had to pay £1,000 for the privilege of being accepted by the society to preside at their function – presumably the Licensed Victuallers Society considered it an honour to be invited and that the firm concerned would receive a lot of useful publicity. When everything was totted up it became quite an expensive evening. Besides the £1,000 donation in this case, wine for the top table and the guests' sprig were expected.

A private entertaining room before the banquet – to which committee members of the association, the president's guests, local dignitaries, including the Lord Mayor, were invited – besides the usual number of gatecrashers – had to be paid for. John Mills the toastmaster – and he also had to be paid for – came up to me in this private room at the Grand telling me that the place had got out of hand and he advised that it should be shut down immediately. He reckoned that it was costing at least £5 a minute.

After the dinner there was another considerable expense. It was customary for the president to dispense hospitality at his table to official and trade guests. The bottles of whisky and gin disappeared at surprising speed. On top of all this, one association insisted that all the ladies should receive a present – needless to say, to be paid for by the president's company.

Nonetheless the Leicester banquet was a success. This was due almost entirely to Lady Barnett, the guest speaker and television personality who was married to a local brewing knight. I got to know Isobel Barnett quite well and we sometimes met up on holidays in Spain. Most regrettably, some years later she took her own life.

On one occasion in Eastbourne, I changed my practice about speeches and got my colleague Francis to draft one. It turned out to be a terrible disaster. Although the content was much better than my usual output it was not my style. Francis had written about lemmings, those small rat-like creatures that tend, from time to time, to jump off cliffs into the sea. I am afraid I got into a bit of a muddle and likened the Eastbourne Licensed Victuallers to a pack of lemmings who were bent on destroying themselves. It did not go down too well.

In spite of my rather derogatory comments about our publican friends I had nothing but warm feelings for that happy band, the Licensed Victuallers Golfing Society. They were an exceptionally good bunch of people, dedicated to the game of golf and good company on the course as well as great companions on 'the nineteenth', at the bar after the day's outing. They were always most generous and hospitable, with their pockets stuffed with notes – presumably nicked from the till before they set off. I once enquired about the amount of ready cash they always seemed to carry around. Bob, a good friend, and a doyen of the society replied that it was 'funny' money. No further questions were asked.

Walkers – probably more than the other whisky firms – sponsored days out on the golf course and provided prizes for the competitors. For many years the main annual outing was at Walton Heath Golf Club, an event originated by Harry Braid, who lived alongside the course and where his father the great James Braid had been the 'pro'. Harry Braid, Arthur Webb and myself, all from the 'old firm', had served their time acting as president of the annual banquet and ball which was latterly held at the Hilton Hotel. It was always a very cheerful occasion with plenty of liquid refreshment.

Another well known event in the Licensed Victuallers Golfing Society's social calender was the annual stag party again held at the Hilton. This was the usual well-attended function at which the wholesale companies entertained friends and guests at their own tables. After a good dinner and light-hearted speeches the highlight of the evening was the cabaret. This entertainment was composed mostly of strippers who were not at all adverse to mingling with the guests and receiving assistance in the removal of their most intimate garments. A friend and myself were none too popular on one occasion by making off with the clothes of a particularly attractive stripper. She, clad only in the very briefest pair of panties, chased us all round the hotel to the amusement of the residents. Back in the ballroom, we finally presented the girl with her frillies to considerable applause. She was a good sport and fortunately took the escapade as a bit of fun. Once dressed again, she joined me and my party for a drink at our table.

18

Playtime

Now chief of the home trade after Arthur's retirement, I settled myself into a fine room in St James's Street. A new drinks cabinet was immediately installed, together with a television set (for the racing) and a few more sporting prints were purchased to adorn the walls. It was a large and gracious room with plenty of space for 'playtime' when business became slack or dull.

Mixed cricket with a squash ball became quite a popular pastime, that is when I was not practising my putting. I always kept my putter and a few balls in a corner of the room and usually took the money if anyone was rash enough to take me on. Being an old building, there was a big 'borrow' which I had learnt to master. One up from us, Justerine & Brooks, the wine merchants, would from time to time indulge in sporting activities from their second-floor office. Their *forte* was making and throwing paper darts. The object was to flight the dart across St James's Street to the other side.

In 1966 my old secretary Gladys reached retirement age and left. She was a grand old soul, having been secretary to John Barr Cumming years ago. Dear old Gladys looked after me like a nanny, producing tea steadily all day and doing her best to keep everyone at arm's length from her boss. I had, however, threatened to fire her on more than one occasion because of her perpetual unpunctuality. More often than not, she would arrive nearer ten am than nine am. Finally, I told her that she had got to go. She started to cry and replied that I would never do that because I was much too kind. Of course, I never did. But, after a temporary improvement, she soon got back into her old ways again.

On her departure at the age of sixty – all the secretaries

seemed to be about that age – I decided it was time for a bit of new blood, and that a young and attractive female would be more appropriate for my needs. Miss J was the first. She came from Yorkshire and was very attractive with a particularly sexy walk. Incidentally, she was bi-lingual (English/French) and most efficient. Miss J completely reorganized my office and had everything at her elegant finger-tips. As with others who succeeded her, visitors multiplied. They would go out of their way to call into the office, where they would be served expertly by a pretty girl, with lots of humour who was ready to talk about anything. Furthermore, they would quite often end up by giving a decent order.

I would sometimes secretly meet up with her at lunchtime or in the evening, surreptitiously, for a drink or supper. In those days it had of necessity to be very much an under-cover operation. If observed by a senior person, both of us would have got the sack forthwith. Attitudes to this sort of thing however, changed greatly a few years on and I like to think I was largely responsible for this.

Our partnership worked happily for three years until one day Miss J announced that she was off to Abidgan on the Ivory Coast. She was getting married and intended to work as a bi-lingual secretary for an oil tycoon. This was a nasty shock and I was unable to get her to change her mind. A number of 'temps' followed who were not really adequate but filled the bill for the time being. Then, one day a young lass, whom I had noticed doing secretarial work for one of my colleagues, strode into my room and announced that she was going to be my secretary.

I was considerably taken aback; but not altogether displeased. Miss P was very pretty with long chestnut brown hair, aged twenty, but looked younger because she usually wore a mini-skirt with socks up to her knees like a child. This ploy was evidently engineered by my colleagues. Following the departure of Miss J, I had become morose and difficult, so my chums decided, with Miss P's approval, that a change of scenery might put me in better humour. It didn't take long before we got on well; this therapeutic treatment had done the trick. I was restored to my usual cheerful and light-hearted manner of doing business.

Miss P was a determined young girl and highly efficient at her work. It took some coaxing for her to mix in with friends and customers and dispense drinks from the cabinet in my room. She worked in a smaller room across the passage and had an intercom buzzer to summon her to her boss's room when I required her. There had been one or two occasions when she had taken a long time to appear – usually when she knew there was a crowd of people in my room. One day when I was on my own, I pressed the buzzer for Miss P to appear. Nothing happened so I kept my finger on the buzzer for about two minutes. Miss P suddenly exploded into the room with a very determined looked. Instead of going to her chair for dictation she came straight round to my side of the large desk, opened the drawer where she knew the buzzer was installed, and proceeded to pull out all the wires. She then did an about turn and strode off out of the room without a word.

I creased myself with laughter, and thought to myself: 'By goodness that girl has got spirit – and she looks damned attractive when she is angry.' At least she won that round and in future I used the internal telephone to summon her. The loose wires remained in the drawer as a memento until my retirement. They are probably still there.

In spite of the traumas – and there were many – the two of us remained good friends. It took a lot of persuasion but Miss P did once accompany me as a reserve driver up to Edinburgh for the start of my fishing holiday on the Dee. She returned by air from Edinburgh airport. Whilst I was fishing the Dee I received a call from Miss P telling me that she had given in her notice. This was another nasty shock. Once more I settled into a state of gloom.

After this unpleasant bit of news my enthusiasm for the fishing holiday waned. Another member of the fishing party, Allan (at that time chairman of Bass) detected that something was wrong and was very sympathetic. He succeeded in extracting the reason for my depression and realized that my marriage was beginning to fall apart. He told me that he had seen me with female company (not my wife) in restaurants on more than one occasion. His advice was: 'Whatever you do, keep a firm base. There will be plenty more.' This second statement indeed proved to be true but his advice, needless to say, went unheeded.

While Tony, the other member of the fishing party, and I were pulling in the odd salmon, try as we might we could not get Allan to land a fish. Every lure – legal or illegal – was resorted to and even the ghillie failed to hook one for him. Such are the vicissitudes, and indeed the charm, of fishing. Allan took it well and made up for things with an extra glass or two or port.

Miss P had stayed for three years which seemed to be about par for the course. Her successor, Miss H, did not hang around. She took over the job like a duck to water and soon made herself perfectly at home. Naturally she was young and attractive: long black hair, this time, with a most agile and acute mind. She was not in the slightest bit interested in whatever other members of the firm thought about her. Her primary job, so far as she was concerned was to keep me happy – both in and out of school.

Miss H's arrival coincided with my divorce – though she was not the reason – and my new bachelor status. From a secure, but unsatisfactory home at Wentworth, I walked out and took a small furnished flat, with a little roof garden, on the top of a large house in Upper Phillimore Gardens, Kensington. Miss H found the flat and indeed she spent more time attending to my problems in the way of accommodation and so forth than she did working for the firm. Soon I was searching around for a more permanent flat to buy. Through friends Miss H came across a recently converted flat in Westbourne Terrace, Bayswater. All the basics had been installed, such as kitchen, bathroom, loos and heating. Otherwise there were just smooth concrete walls.

Miss H arranged for the painting and decoration of the whole flat with her own colour schemes with the exception of the main hall passage, which I insisted must be bright red. She had *carte blanche* at Aspreys, Harrods, Goodes & Heals to furnish and fit out the place. At that time I had no furniture, beds, linen, cooking utensils, crockery or cutlery – all my possessions were stuck at Wentworth. The flat ended up by being particularly attractive and easy to run, with an excellent daily to look after the place.

During this interim period , Miss H, in her business-like and efficient way, was invaluable. As a reward I took her to Paris to watch the Arc de Triomphe race. Later on we had a number of short jaunts in Europe. She was a good driver and enjoyed it. We visited châteaux on the Loire, Brittany and Normandy to sample the excellent food and at the same time to visit the war grave of my elder brother. Taking a slightly extended Easter holiday we also took a memorable trip to Luxembourg and Salzburg via Brussels through the Alsace wine-growing country on to Germany and ending up in Berne, Switzerland. Miss H was fluent in French and could carry on a conversation in German. Alas, all good things come to an end and she decided to leave, having fixed up an extended holiday to Greece.

The next girl to appear on the scene was Miss E from 'Appy 'Ampstead. She was a very attractive redhead with a good sense of humour and well qualified in all secretarial duties, a good time-keeper and punctilious in every way. No wonder – her father had been chief of police in Jamaica, Barbados and other West Indian countries. Miss E had just got married when the interview for the job took place and indeed I myself was to get hitched up again only a few months afterwards. Miss E later told me that the initial interview was one of the most extraordinary experiences she had ever had. On entering my very spacious room she spied me at the far end seated at the biggest desk she had ever seen. There was nothing on it, apart from three telephones and a blotter. As she padded across the carpet she thought I looked like 'a little gnome'. I invited her to sit on the chair opposite.

It is very difficult to interview a pretty girl, who you have never seen before and you only have a sketchy knowledge of what her duties are. Apparently my opening line went something like this: 'My goodness you *have* got a lot of freckles. Are you always like that or have you just come back from a holiday?'

Miss E, rather surprised, replied that it was a bit of each. We went on to talk about holidays in general and had an interesting chat about the West Indies, where she was brought up. Indeed at one stage she was selected to swim for the Bahamas against a team of Americans in Florida and she won. I thought to myself: 'By goodness we have got something here,' and I felt it would be nice to continue the conversation over a drink. I directed her to the drinks cabinet where she fixed a very good whisky with soda and ice and we continued to talk. By this stage I had practically got her life history out of her. After about an hour's pleasant conversation evidently I felt I should ask her something about work.

According to Miss E's own account of this interview, I then directed her back to the large desk where I sat down in quite a business-like manner. She reports that I then said: 'Can you type?' She was nonplussed at this, having been to secretarial college and used the services of the director's secretaries agency for the interview. She laughed heartily and secretly thought to herself: 'The stupid old bugger, what's going to come next.' Yet she was entertained.

I was not aware that she had already been screened and tested by Peter, the 'admin' man, on shorthand and typing and had proved to be 'A1'. The interview over, I took her along to show her the typewriter and files and introduce her to the secretary she was taking over from, who would explain things. There was no-one there and the typewriter was covered up. Evidently the girl had taken the afternoon off to go out shopping – at least that was what I *thought* must have happened.

Taking Miss E to the lift to see her off, I said: 'Are you coming here?'

She replied: 'Yes, I think you could do with a bit of organizing'.

Miss E proved to be a very good selection and she remained with me for some years – in fact until the year before I retired, when she had a baby. Our two families saw lot of each other and often joined forces for the opera at Covent Garden. Indeed we went on holiday together to the Greek Islands, the Algarve and Italy. I was able to confirm that she was a brilliant swimmer: she shot through the water like a shark.

The get-together arranged for Miss E's leaving party in my room at Walkers was memorable. All the home trade staff were present together with some of the export directors and Hugh, Miss E's husband. I presented her with a leaving present and, as is customary, said a few words. In fact, it was probably the best speech I ever made. I had no difficulty in extolling her virtues and I recounted the humorous incidents that had occurred over the past nine years. Hugh was greatly entertained and remarked afterwards that I 'Might have been talking about a *wife* rather than a secretary'.

Miss E's response was hilarious – never before had it been known for a member of staff, let alone a very attractive secretary, to take the mickey out of her boss to the extent she did. The export directors were open-mouthed yet highly amused by the familiarity between the two of us, and they laughed heartily about the incidents that had occurred during 'playtime' in the afternoons. Miss E ended her speech by saying: 'When I have left, be kind to the Old Fool. If you ever find him wandering around the passages in a bemused way take him by the arm and lead him back to his playpen!'

Just before Miss E left I was delighted to be introduced to Miss Jo, a 'temp' who Peter, the admin man, felt would be a suitable replacement. She was a delightful girl and a real stunner. She fitted into my strange way of life admirably and was always perfectly at home with friends and customers who were always dropping into my office. She dispensed drinks and chatted them up. Although Miss Jo was only supposed to work with me as a 'temp' for a few weeks she remained for a year until my retirement. Her parents lived on Barra, one of the outer isles off Scotland, so I gave her a fishing rod as a parting present.

In my capacity as home sales director, I was very much into the racing syndrome. The firm had boxes at Ascot and Epsom, for which I was responsible, and they also sponsored a number of races – in particular the Johnnie Walker Ebor at York. There were also important sponsored races at Ayr and Lingfield, where excellent parties were given for the trade and other guests. From these activities and my attendance at many other meetings in a business or social capacity I got to know the racing fraternity, trainers and jockeys, quite well. So it was a fairly natural progression that I should own a horse.

Through Stan, and the firm's distributor in Nigeria and already a considerable owner, a yearling was bought in Ireland. The journalist Richard Behrens (William Hickey) of the *Daily Express* had the other 'leg'. It was decided to call the horse The Hughstan and it was registered as such. The horse was sent to Epsom to be trained by John Sutcliffe, who already trained a string of horses for Stan. This stage in the ownership of the horse was fun. The three owners would go down to the stables on Sunday to look at the animals, particularly The Hughstan, be well entertained at John's house, and end up by having a good lunch at the Fairmile Hotel, Cobham. We were all hopeful and quite optimistic about the future running of the horse. Indeed later on, John even advised us that The Hughstan was to be entered for the 2,000 Guineas. Alas, this was not to be.

The horse grew bigger and bigger. It was over seventeen hands as a two-year old and it grew so tall they could only just get it out of its box. Although friendly enough, it was a strange-looking animal. It had flop ears and appeared to have a form or string halt in its hind legs. The lad had the greatest difficulty in getting the horse to trot when showing him off to the owners. The Hughstan did not seem to like the daylight too much and preferred to get back to his box to rest. Needless to say, he did *not* run as a two-year old as anticipated and due to a variety of ailments he did not even set foot on a racecourse until he was four. Because of his size, his legs were none too good, so he was 'fired'. The next problem was his breathing. He used to blow on the rare occasion when he took any exercise so he was despatched to Newmarket for an operation for soft palate.

By now it was realized that The Hughstan would not be much good on the flat. He was eating his head off at a first class trainer's with no prospect of getting a race into him, so it was decided to transfer him to a small trainer for half the price. The position was not dissimilar to a layabout living at the Ritz when his rightful home should be at a boarding house. The new trainer considered that the only option open to The Hughstan was to put him to jumping. So he was gelded and trained 'over the sticks'. The Hughstan was eventually entered in a small hurdle race as a four-year old. He came in last.

The horse was then rested for a year and given a final opportunity in another small hurdle race as a five-year old. Although he got round he ended up lame; the jockey reported that he 'blew like a whale'. A hasty meeting was arranged and it was reluctantly decided that the poor old horse had to be put down. From great expectations The Hughstan more than likely ended up as tinned dog food. The one and only cheque the owners actually *received* was from the knacker's yard. Such are the uncertainties of owning a race horse.

19

The Bubble Bursts

Besides day-to-day business with Johnnie Walker's and the odd frolic, I now found myself with plenty on my plate. The income from the family mills in Bradford was declining. New tenants were hard to come by such old-fashioned property and the cost of maintenance and repair became alarmingly high. With the other trustees' agreement, I decided to sell up.

This was sad, but inevitable. The property was only worth a fairly modest amount, but over the years, thanks to my insistence, a healthy reserve had been built up consisting of stocks and shares. At least, instead of a regular income, all the beneficiaries received a nice little nest egg and they seemed to be content.

And apart from the winding up of the Bradford estate I was busy with my farming enterprise in Shropshire. The Heath Farm of some four hundred acres became vacant, too, so I decided to take it over. This presented problems with regard to finding sufficient funds for stocking the farm, buying implements and machines and modernizing some of the old buildings. I achieved this by selling the Twitchen, the little farm I had begun with, and also another outlying tenanted farm. But the most important decision was the selection of an honest up-to-date reliable farm manager. As I was away in London most of the time, it was essential to find the right man for the job.

I was fortunate in obtaining the services of Tom, who went to live in the farm house. The two of us got along very well indeed and built up this rather neglected and run-down farm into a viable operation. Fine new cattle sheds were erected and a grain-dryer was installed. As more of a hobby than a commercial operation I persuaded Tom to build up a herd of pedigree polled Herefords. This proved to be quite successful and some young bulls were sold profitably. One was sold to a farmer in the Isle of Coll in the outer isles of Scotland, where he became a stud bull. A load of heifers was also shipped to Italy, so I was doing my bit in the export field.

Finance was always a problem, but in this respect I was in a happier position than some. At least I was able to exist on my salary from the whisky firm so profits were ploughed back into the business. I refused to borrow in spite of pressure from Tom. Of course, there were the usual farming overdrafts, but the situation was usually corrected after the harvest.

However, my interference on one occasion cost the farm a bit of money and ended up in disaster. Feeling that the large new cattle sheds should be utilized during the summer months, when the beasts were out grazing in the meadows, I suggested that they should be filled with young pigs to be fattened up. Hundreds of hogs were bought from all over the place. They presented quite an unusual sight. All seemed to be going well until some of them began to get sick. The trouble came to a head when a batch was sent off for sale at Craven Arms. One little pig was put on the scales and it collapsed. A vet was called and it was found that it had swine fever. This caused a terrible furore in the market place. Back on the farm, all the pigs had to be slaughtered straight away. There was no compensation. Furthermore the farm had to be completely isolated for the next few weeks – police and officials were everywhere. It was my first and last venture into pigs.

The other problem was my marriage to Dot. Although we had had a happy relationship for many years, rows and quarrels now seemed to be breaking out more and more frequently. Maybe it was my fault to some extent. I had always been a bit of a philanderer and perhaps a succession of pretty secretaries was a contributory cause. I was also, I had to admit, partial to the product I sold and would quite frequently arrive home late, often rather the worse for wear.

I had resolved, some years previously, that I would never break up the marriage until the children, Caroline and William, had reached their teens. Then, after issuing one or two threats to leave, I decided to get divorced at any price. One Sunday afternoon I was discovered by Dot in my dressing room at Wentworth packing a large suitcase. I told her I was off. I had had enough. She helped me pack – quite a poignant situation – and I left that afternoon for the little flat in Upper Phillimore Gardens.

Dot's parting words were: 'You will regret this. I will take you for everything you have got . . . .' And she jolly nearly did.

Yet although upsetting at the time, it was a well-thought out operation and, in the end, it turned out that there were no regrets.

After protracted meetings with lawyers, it was agreed that, by way of a settlement, I would hand over to Dot one thousand acres in Shropshire. This included the four hundred acre farm in hand, together with all the equipment and stock. Dot was not prepared to have the property tied up in any way, yet there was a 'gentleman's agreement' that she would live off the income and, in due time, hand the estate over to the children. But she was to have other thoughts about that.

Having reached agreement over the settlement, it was now time to put into operation a cause for divorce and this would, inevitably, be adultery. I was put in touch with a retired solicitor who specialized in this type of business. A rather sleazy hotel in Basil Street was decided upon and a date was arranged for me to stay two nights with a female to be provided by the solicitor. I had visions of a pretty nubile companion with everything provided for me on a plate. I was looking forward to the encounter. The day arrived and I booked in with the doorman and general *factotum* – a crafty looking man with a hunchback and a limp, who proved to be the key witness. I was shown up to the bedroom, which contained one large double bed and little else.

I had been advised that the lady would arrive at about seven pm so I was all agog and awaiting the knock on the door with great anticipation. She arrived on time and was ushered in by the hunchback. I then received one of the biggest shocks of my life. Instead of a beautiful young blonde she turned out to be a scraggy middle-aged cow with bad breath and a very nasty cold.

How to escape was my immediate reaction. So I made a deal: I suggested that the old bag should go away and return at midnight whilst I would go off to my club. I planned to get very drunk until we met at the witching hour. I only have a very hazy recollection of our night together. I was woken up by snorts and grunts from time to time until the hunchback appeared in the morning with a pot of tea. He duly obtained the evidence required but in case there was any hitch in court, I was advised that two nights with the lady would be foolproof.

So the 'co-respondent' and I agreed to part until midnight the next night. On my return to the scruffy hotel at midnight, suitably inebriated, I met my companion in the hall; she was chatting to the hunchback. It was now that I took pity on the wretched female and I decided to offer her a drink. We stayed up drinking and talking until the early hours. She turned out to be a pretty decent soul and evidently made her living, using a variety of assumed names, in this unusual type of occupation.

Next morning, the hunchback appeared again with a pot of tea. My bedmate assured me that I need take no further action. When the hearing took place she and the hunchback would give evidence and there was no necessity for me to be present in the court. This indeed happened. We parted good friends.

Following the divorce, my life, based on my comfortable flat in Westbourne Terrace, took on an enjoyable new flavour. I was not short of female friends.

Life in the whisky world went on much as usual and out of hours I became quite a regular visitor to Annabel's and the Stork Club. At this time I used to drive around London in my car and had one or two scrapes with the police over excess of alcohol.

Once, when visiting Royal Mid-Surrey Golf Course for lunch with some friends and golf afterwards, there was a deluge so it was decided to play billiards instead. Having lunched well, decanters of port arrived at regular intervals. But as the afternoon wore on one of the party, an eminent broadcasting friend, was missing. After a search he was found fast asleep in the boot of his Jaguar. It emerged that he had decided to transfer his clubs from the club house to his car and, being rather the worse for wear, he fell into the boot with them. Sensibly he ordered a car to take him home.

By this stage I was in a similar condition and yet I had to drive back to London for a date. Sure enough, I had only gone a few miles – steering an unsteady course – when I was stopped and breathalysed. Inevitably, I was over the top so I was conducted to Kingston nick in a police car. On arrival I asked for a glass of water which they were kind enough to give me.

They also allowed me to use the telephone to tell Susie that I would be late for our date.

A very severe and senior policewoman now entered the room and, after a few cautionary words, the breathalyser apparatus was put into operation again. For some extraordinary reason, the result was *negative* so I was in the clear and allowed to go. My car had been brought back to the police station and so, having asked instructions from the sergeant as to how to get out of the place and back to London, I started the engine. I proceeded to drive straight into a wall. The kindly sergeant, who had been in attendance all along, remarked: 'Don't press your luck *too far*, Sir – get on home.' I did so, at high speed and without incident.

My other notable encounter with the police occurred in the early hours of the morning after a particularly heavy night. On arriving home I found I had locked my keys inside. I decided to try to stay with my secretary Miss E and her husband in Hampstead. The trouble was that I did not know how to find their flat although I had the address in my diary. In a very merry state I set off for Hampstead. On the way I observed a police car on a main thoroughfare around Swiss Cottage which had pulled in alongside another motorist. I drew up next to the police car, more or less in the middle of the road, and breezily asked if they could help me find an address nearby.

They were courteous, if a little surprised, and wanted to know the circumstances. I explained that I had locked myself out. After a few moments one of the officers said: 'You have had a good evening – you smell like a *brewery*. What's your occupation?' I replied that I was a distiller. Whereupon the officers said: 'For Christ's sake get your car off this road and park up that side road.'

I indicated that I wasn't keen to do that because they might desert me. The officers assured me they would come along when they were finished with the other motorist. To my relief the police car duly arrived and they asked me to get in with them, saying they would take me to the address I wanted. On the short journey I overheard the one say to the other: 'By goodness we have got a *right one* here'.

They were a couple of really decent young coppers. They were out to help whereas they might easily have arrested me. I insisted they escorted me to the upstairs flat where I rung the bell. Hugh answered the door with Miss E, in her nightdress, lurking behind. They both looked thoroughly shaken and apprehensive. It was about three o'clock in the morning by this time. They had the impression that I was handcuffed and had committed some terrible crime. But all's well that ends well and so I spent the rest of the night in their spare bedroom.

The next morning, before work, Miss E and I went to collect the car, but there was no sign of it where I thought I had parked the blasted banger. After a two hour search it was discovered up some little side street nowhere near where I thought I had left it.

When Johnnie Walker Red Label was going strong and just about at the top of the sales league the managing director expressed a wish to have a series of receptions in England and Scotland to get to know the trade. These parties were known amongst the home trade as 'DCK see the people'.

My co-director Francis fixed up each reception in magnificent style and always in some original setting. For example, he took over Cardiff Castle for a fine evening reception with a Welsh lady playing the harp in the background. On another occasion he hired Lord Montagu's seat at Beaulieu for a reception with, this time, medieval musicians in the background.

I was staying at the Montagu Arms at Beaulieu for this function. This is a distinguished, old-fashioned hotel with some fine pieces of furniture. As was customary, all the guests and the hosts partook liberally of Scotch whisky besides good wines for dinner. By bedtime I was in a happy state, having consumed my usual sort of quota. My large bedroom had a distinctly sloping floor with a huge tallboy, leaning inwards, dominating the far wall. On approaching the tallboy in order to put away my clothes, I was horrified to see this top-heavy piece of furniture moving towards me. There was a resounding crash and I found myself pinned beneath the bloody thing. Struggle as I might, I could not wriggle my way out. What seemed an eternity elapsed until one of my colleagues in an adjacent room heard my painful cries and came to the rescue.

At this time there had been a lot of turmoil in the trade about price cutting and Walkers were just as guilty in this respect as others. The problem stemmed from the fact that there were two prices – one for the home trade and the other, a higher price, for distributors in continental Europe. This had been a historical way of doing things, ensuring a decent profit for both the producer and the distributor. It had always been the policy of the firm to allow the distributor a good margin to enable him to run an efficient sales force and to contribute towards advertising and special promotions.

Meanwhile, many of the British traders, with their price advantage, started what was termed a 'parallel business'. This meant that they sold direct to continental supermarkets or to fringe middle-men who circumvented the established trade through the *bona fide* distributors. Although the miscreants were put on a 'stop' list and incurred penalties, this type of business still continued. It caused chaos in the continental markets and a loss of profit to the distributors. There had been rumblings for some time from the EEC in Brussels about the dual-pricing structure which they complained was an infringement of the Treaty of Rome. This, together with restrictions imposed by the firm on the British parallel traders, resulted in a court case at Strasbourg.

Walkers were found guilty of breaking the rules. It was understood, that, unless the firm abandoned the dual-pricing structure, they would be liable for a huge fine. All Scotch whisky firms with a home and export trade were in a similar position, but presumably Walkers were taken to task because Red Label was far and away the biggest seller in Europe and consequently the British parallel exporters (the miscreants) found a ready market there.

The upshot of this tricky situation was unfortunate for me. Whilst there were a number of options open to the top management of the group it was decided to stop sales of Red Label entirely in the United Kingdom, the home trade, until a successful appeal had been lodged in the Strasbourg Court. The *bona fide* export trade of Red Label continued and continental distributors resumed their historical and successful role without interruption from the cowboys.

The upshot was that I and my home trade sales team now entered into quite a different ball game. From sales of more than a million cases *per annum* we now had nothing to sell other than Black Label and our malt whisky Cardhu.

It was a costly and brave decision to take. Time will tell whether it was the correct one. Certainly in the short term it stopped the rot.

As a replacement for Red Label a new brand called John Barr was introduced. I suggested the name myself and it was accepted by the board. John Barr Cumming had been my first managing director way back in 1947 and was responsible for my joining the firm.

In order to get the show on the road, a series of tastings and receptions were given in big towns in England, Scotland and Wales. Advertising and PR played their part. It was discovered that it was not easy to introduce a new brand in spite of having friendly relations with the trade. There was no question of John Barr taking over from Red Label in a similar volume.

Brewers and wine and spirit merchants were ready enough to give initial orders, but follow-up orders were not as good as anticipated. The general public knew nothing about the brand and there were a lot of 'unknowns' on the market. Besides EEC restrictions dictated that the new brand should bear no resemblance whatsoever to Red Label, either in the get-up or in the blend itself. After all Red Label had been going strong since 1820.

But none the less the sales of John Barr were by no means disastrous. There were certain pockets around the country, particularly Scotland, where it did very well. At least it was good fun bashing around the countryside with the sales team promoting the new stuff – even if sometimes a bit exhausting and tough on the liver. It was a nice change for Miss E to get out of the office and help with arrangements and chat up the customers. A little female persuasion often yielded dividends.

The appeal to the court ruling dragged on for years and I had retired by the time Red Label was happily reintroduced to the home market.

20

Still Going Strong

After my divorce from Dot I had no particular thought of remarriage. I was content enough in my flat in Westbourne Terrace living a happy-go-lucky life. Women came and went and I was happy enough with the situation.

I was fortunate in securing the services of an excellent daily, strangely enough with the name of Mrs Bird. Realizing my inadequacies on the domestic scene, she took me in hand and kept the place in apple-pie order.

Yet I often found myself rather irritated and frustrated by the behaviour of my female companions. Generally they proved to be unreliable and tended to let me down; and it was a nuisance trying to find a replacement at short notice.

One day my friend Sonja, whom I had known for years, and who, since my divorce often accompanied me to trade functions in London, telephoned me. She asked me to a party she was throwing at her house in Tite Street. I arrived at the appointed house in a large chauffeur-driven limousine, hot and sweaty after a day's golf at the Berkshire Club. Unbeknown to me, she had invited, amongst many others, a girl whom she thought would hit it off with me. She felt it would be a suitable introduction.

Towards the end of the party, and after chatting up various people, I noticed a female who looked outstanding and seemed to show good form. I decided to move in and have a word with her. She was as brown as a nut and her nose was peeling. I discovered that she had just returned with a chance acquaintance in a Lamborghini from Majorca, stopping off at Paris. This was impressive.

Susie, for that was her name, had come to the party with three of her holiday Majorcan friends – Tony, 'Little Hugh' and 'Tom Cat'. They were quite happy when Susie told them she was going off to dinner with the new bloke she had just met.

I dismissed the huge limousine still waiting in Tite Street – Susie providing the tip – and we set off for a nearby restaurant in her car. After an amusing dinner, I discovered that I had no cash on me so she paid the bill. Then she drove me home to Westbourne Terrace – much out of her way. I tried to inveigle her into my flat, but she would have none of it. At least I telephoned her up in Putney later that night to find out if she had got back safely.

I married Susie in 1972 and we moved into my bachelor flat in Westbourne Terrace. Our daughter Kate arrived in 1974. Soon the place, with 'Jackie' the nanny, became too small for us all.

One day, before setting off for a business trip to Ireland, I suggested that Susie should pull her finger out and find a *house*, preferably freehold for us all to live in. On my return I had a bad tummy and was closeted in the loo. I remember frantic knocks on the door accompanied by shouts to the effect that Susie had bought a house. With more urgent matters to attend to, I merely replied: 'OK, fine'.

The house in Abingdon Villas, Kensington, turned out to be in appalling condition and I had quite a shock when I saw it. Jackie thought it was the most awful place she had ever seen. The builders and decorators moved in for a stint of at least six months; but it proved to be a shrewd buy. We have now lived there for a good dozen years, each owning half the house and have no intention of leaving.

I retired from Johnnie Walker's in 1981 at the age of sixty-five. Now, apart from some involvement in underwriting at Lloyd's and the supervision of my greatly reduced agricultural property in Shropshire, I do nothing. I am perfectly content with this state of affairs.

My retirement parties given by the drink trade were memorable; but unfortunately the last one ended in disaster. In high spirits after a session at Annabel's I ran up the stairs two at a time and missed my footing. I keeled over backwards, landing on my head on the marble floor. I passed out in a pool of blood and had to be carted off to Westminster Hospital in an ambulance. A nasty cut on my forehead was stitched up and I suffered from concussion – not to mention a hangover.

The doctor visiting me the next day mentioned that he had had trouble sewing up the cut on my head. He had difficulty getting the needle through the skin. It transpired that the needle had hit a bit of shrapnel – the result of a war wound over forty years previously.

The agricultural property given by way of a settlement to Dot was – as anticipated – broken up and sold for a large amount of money. A small business expansion scheme company bought the property (just in time, as the law was changed soon afterwards) and other bits were bought by sitting tenants. A good chunk of the sale proceeds went to the tax man but some gifts were made to Caroline and William. She was always most generous to the children. So at least Dot achieved her threat and took me to the cleaners.

Yet all is not lost in Shropshire. I and my family have a great affection for its countryside. When staying up there we live at The Oak, a smallholding house on the estate, which at one time was a pub – and consequently has a fine cellar.

Kate, now in her teens, has developed into a good fisherman and the two of us spend many happy hours fishing for trout in nearby ponds.